Monkey

中国十二生肖运程全集与风水调理

**KNOWLEDGE OF
THE TWELVE ANIMAL SIGNS
AND PRACTICES OF
CHINESE FENG-SHUI THEORY**

猴

D1042758

Monkey people: wary and active people.

Climbing, jumping, and pursuing, they have fulfilled

J   This is Monkey people.

目录 CONTENTS

1　Lunar Calendar and Solar Calendar in China　/6

2　The Law of Chinese *Yin-Yang* and *Wuxing* /8

3　Legend of the Monkey　/10

4　Personalities of Monkey People　/12

5　Fate and Wealth Luck of Monkey People　/14

6　Love and Marriage of Monkey People　/16

7　Careers of Monkey People　/18

8　Specification of the Five Elements for Monkey People　/20

9　Monkey People and the Twelve Constellations　/32

10　Fate of Monkey People Born in Different Hours　/58

11　Fate of Monkey People in the Twelve Animal Years　/62

12　Monkey People's Tutelary God and Animal Year　/76

13　Monkey People's *Feng-Shui* Mascots Related with the Five Elements　/78

14　Divinatory Symbols of One's Animal Year and Eight Kinds of Divinatory Symbols of Buildings　/81

15　Auspicious *Feng-Shui* Orientations and Typical *Feng-Shui* Mascots　/86

16　How to Hold and Rearrange One's Fate　/102

前言
Preface

The ten Heavenly Stems and the twelve Earthly Branches (*Gan-Zhi* in Chinese) were originally used to designate years before the Christian era was adopted in China. *Gan* represents *Jia, Yi, Bing, Ding, Wu, Ji, Geng, Xin, Ren, Gui,* (it is a way to rank sequences by Chinese words.) thus is also called the ten Heavenly Stems; while *Zhi* represents *Zi, Chou, Yin, Mao, Chen, Si, Wu, Wei, Shen, You, Xu,* and *Hai,* thus is also called the twelve Earthly Branches.

Gan-Zhi is too abstract to remember, especially for those people that haven't received much education. As a result, twelve animals were selected to match the twelve Earthly Branches. For example, *Zi* Rat, *Chou* Ox, *Yin* Tiger, *Mao* Rabbit, *Chen* Dragon, *Si* Snake, *Wu* Horse, *Wei* Goat, *Shen* Monkey, *You* Rooster, *Xu* Dog, and *Hai* Pig. These are the twelve Animal Signs, also called the twelve *Shengxiao* in Chinese.

There are Five Elements for each Animal Sign in every 60 years. For example, in 60 years, *Shen* Monkey consists of five categories including Metal *Shen* Monkey, Wood *Shen* Monkey, Water *Shen* Monkey, Fire *Shen* Monkey, and Earth *Shen* Monkey. Since each Animal Sign has five different categories, there are totally 60 species of the twelve Animal Signs in 60

十二生肖：向上封侯

Becoming a marquis.

years. The odd and even of the ten Heavenly Stems and the twelve Earthly Branches match each other, designating years in the order of *Jia-Zi, Yi-Chou, Bing-Yin,* etc. Every 60 years is a circulation and called one "60 *Jia-Zi*" era.

The divinity monkey indicating longevity.

It was in the Eastern Han Dynasty, about 1800 years ago, that the twelve Animal Signs were completely recorded in Wang Chong's *Lun Heng* (Discourses Weighed in the Balance). This book indicates that even early in the Eastern Han Dynasty, the twelve Animal Signs were used to designate years.

Later, the twelve Animal Signs gradually evolved into the Chinese traditional culture and went deep into Chinese people's hearts. Endowed with a kind of supernatural power and inosculated with *Wuxing* identifications (the Five Elements of Metal, Wood, Water, Fire, and Earth), *Yin-Yang* theory, and *Zhouyi* theory which is a famous Feng-Shui book for predicting one's fate in China three thousand years ago, the knowledge of the twelve Animal Signs further evolved into *Shengxiao* theory, which, as an old Chinese culture, is appreciated and regarded highly by Chinese and overseas scholars. The knowledge of the twelve Animal Signs is an important part not only of Chinese traditional culture, but also of the international folk-customs.

Feng-Shui mascot monkey for longevity.

Feng-Shui mascot monkey for happiness.

1 中国阴历与阳历
Lunar Calendar and Solar Calendar in China

Solar calendar is also called *Taiyang* calendar in Chinese, in regard to the time that the earth circles one detour around the sun as one year. It is commonly used by western countries, and also called the Western Calendar. China adopted solar calendar in 1912.

Lunar calendar is also called *Taiyin* calendar in Chinese, in regard to the time that the moon circles one detour around the earth as one month, and one detour around the sun with the earth as one year. As a matter of fact, it also adopts solar calendar for reference. Lunar calendar was used in China before 1912.

Now, it is the solar calendar that is primarily used in China, assisted with the lunar calendar as a reference. Main Chinese folk custom festivals and the twelve Animal Signs are according to the lunar calendar.

Chinese Confucianism: Look not at what is contrary to propriety, listen not to what is contrary to propriety, speak not what is contrary to propriety.

120 年五行属相编年表
The List of the Five Elements During a Period of 120 Years in the Gregorian Calendar

RAT	1924	1936	1948	1960	1972	1984	1996	2008	2020	2032
	Metal	Water	Fire	Earth	Wood	Metal	Water	Fire	Earth	Wood
OX	1925	1937	1949	1961	1973	1985	1997	2009	2021	2033
	Metal	Water	Fire	Earth	Wood	Metal	Water	Fire	Earth	Wood
TIGER	1926	1938	1950	1962	1974	1986	1998	2010	2022	2034
	Fire	Earth	Wood	Metal	Water	Fire	Earth	Wood	Metal	Water
RABBIT	1927	1939	1951	1963	1975	1987	1999	2011	2023	2035
	Fire	Earth	Wood	Metal	Water	Fire	Earth	Wood	Metal	Water
DRAGON	1928	1940	1952	1964	1976	1988	2000	2012	2024	2036
	Wood	Metal	Water	Fire	Earth	Wood	Metal	Water	Fire	Earth
SNAKE	1929	1941	1953	1965	1977	1989	2001	2013	2025	2037
	Wood	Metal	Water	Fire	Earth	Wood	Metal	Water	Fire	Earth
HORSE	1930	1942	1954	1966	1978	1990	2002	2014	2026	2038
	Earth	Wood	Metal	Water	Fire	Earth	Wood	Metal	Water	Fire
GOAT	1931	1943	1955	1967	1979	1991	2003	2015	2027	2039
	Earth	Wood	Metal	Water	Fire	Earth	Wood	Metal	Water	Fire
MONKEY	1932	1944	1956	1968	1980	1992	2004	2016	2028	2040
	Metal	Water	Fire	Earth	Wood	Metal	Water	Fire	Earth	Wood
ROOSTER	1933	1945	1957	1969	1981	1993	2005	2017	2029	2041
	Metal	Water	Fire	Earth	Wood	Metal	Water	Fire	Earth	Wood
DOG	1934	1946	1958	1970	1982	1994	2006	2018	2030	2042
	Fire	Earth	Wood	Metal	Water	Fire	Earth	Wood	Metal	Water
PIG	1935	1947	1959	1971	1983	1995	2007	2019	2031	2043
	Fire	Earth	Wood	Metal	Water	Fire	Earth	Wood	Metal	Water

2 中国阴阳五行的运行规律
The Law of Chinese *Yin-Yang* and *Wuxing*

The ancient Chinese abstracted the relations between human beings and the universe into the Five Elements including Metal, Wood, Water, Fire, and Earth. It is taken for granted that the universe consisted of the Five Elements. The change of each element grows *Yin* and *Yang*. *Yin* and *Yang* are the different principles complementing and counteracting with each other. The relations between *Yin* and *Yang* represent the general developing rules of everything in the universe.

The complementary relations indicate that the Five Elements could complement and enhance with each other: Metal enhances Water; Water enhances Wood; Wood enhances Fire; Fire enhances Earth; Earth enhances Metal.

The counteractive relations indicate that the Five Elements would counteract with each other: the Metal counteracts the Water; the Water counteracts the Wood; the Wood counteracts the Fire; the Fire counteracts the Earth; the Earth counteracts the Metal.

Ancient Chinese people thought that *Yin-Yang* and the Five Elements, together with the twelve Earthly Branches constitute a "*Jia-Zi*" era. They found that once born, every person has certain regular fate that circulates in every 60 years and could be forecasted according to the theory about "60 *Jia-Zi*" era.

Invested with marquis.

The golden monkey bringing good luck.

3 猴的属相传说
Legend of the Monkey

The monkey is one kind of the mammalian of Primates, including the wild monkey, the spider monkey, the long-nose monkey, the golden monkey and so on. The Monkey ranks the ninth in the twelve Zodiac Animal Signs, and it corresponds with the ninth of the twelve Earthly Branches-*Shen*. So *Shen* hour, the period of the day from 3 p.m. to 5 a.m., can also be called "Monkey hour".

How comes your Animal Sign Monkey?

As the saying goes "the monkey reigns in the mountains when the tiger is out", obviously, the tiger was considered as the king of beasts by the people in ancient times; while the monkey, due to its astuteness, also got a position in people's minds. In fact, there did exist a deep fellowship between tiger and monkey. It is said that monkey succeeded to be one of the twelve Animal Signs largely because of tiger's help.

According to the legend, the tiger had been the king of beasts for its prestige as the ruler of the mountains since the very beginning. All the beasts in the mountains would shy away once they met the tiger. The tiger felt satisfied as well as lonely. At that time, the monkey was the neighbor of the tiger. They called each other brother and were in extremely close relationship. Later, the monkey became the tiger's right hand. When the Tiger King went out, the monkey would rule the mountains on behalf of the Tiger King, and all the beasts had to follow the monkey's orders because they were afraid of the Tiger King. This was how the saying came into being. One day, the Tiger King fell into the hunter's trap unluckily. It tried very hard to escape; however, it didn't succeed to do so. It so happened that the monkey was passing by, so the Tiger King asked for help. Seeing this, the monkey immediately climbed onto the tree, released the ropes and saved the tiger.

Out of danger, the Tiger King thanked its monkey brother many times. However, in its mind it had different ideas. It thought: "I am the king of beasts. Unexpectedly I fell into the hunter's trap, and was rescued by the small monkey. If the monkey makes it public, it will certainly do damage to my portliness as the King. I'd better get rid of it." However, it had a second thought then: "I am already a loner, if I kill the monkey; I will have no friend any more. Then who will come to help me if I am in danger again? Besides, the monkey dares not to give mouth to what happened today because it is afraid of me."

So the tiger told the monkey: "I will repay you for your kindness of saving my life. In the future, if you have any trouble, you can count on my help." The monkey of course didn't mention one word about the whole incident in order to keep the King's face. From then on, the two had a more extraordinary relationship.

Many years later, the Heaven Emperor began to choose the Animal Signs. As the king of beasts, the tiger naturally became an Animal Sign. The monkey heard the news and wanted to be an Animal Sign too. But the Heaven Emperor's principle of choosing the Animal Signs was that the animal should have made great contributions to mankind. But the monkey hadn't done much to mankind, so it was unqualified.

The monkey turned to the Tiger King for help. It asked the Tiger King to go to the Heaven Emperor and ask for a favor so that the monkey can be selected as an Animal Sign. Since the tiger owed its life to the monkey, it had to ask for a favor for the monkey from the Heaven Emperor. He told the Heaven Emperor the monkey was the most intelligent animal among all the beasts. He also mentioned that the monkey had made great contributions by ruling the mountains when he was away. So the Heaven Emperor ordered that the monkey was also listed as an Animal Sign. Finally the monkey was chosen to be an Animal Sign and the Tiger King repaid the monkey's kindness. Certainly, the Tiger King was unhappy because the monkey, who had no special skills, was together with it listed as an Animal Sign. As a result, the friendship of the two broke off. Today, none of beasts are afraid of the money any more. Accordingly, the saying "the monkey reigns in the mountains when the tiger is out", which once reflected the truth, gradually gains its sarcastic meaning.

4 属猴人性格
Personalities of Monkey People

The people born in the Monkey year are open, energetic, smart, versatile, and flexible. They are competitive and smart in handling things. Also they are chivalrous and always ready to help others even they have to put aside their own affairs. They should pay special attention to this in order to achieve successes. The people born in the Monkey year are tolerant and generous. The females born in the Monkey year are lucky in their first marriages, and endurable and consistent.

The people born in the Monkey year are smart. They are agile in reaction, outstanding in talents and can easily attract others' attention. They like doing everything by themselves and being the leaders of a group. They are flighty and anxious in actions, and usually speak with biting sarcasm. As a result, they easily arouse others' antipathy. Regarded highly, they may be envied by other people because they are so eager to show their talents. They should endeavor constantly, avoid showing temper by all means and be patient and persistent. Only by doing this can they pave the way for successes.

Monkey people will have a few friends and followers in spite of their flirtation because they are willing to help others. When they meet difficulties, their good friends will help them.

中国福利彩票
面值贰元　增值无效
猴戏
中国福利彩票发行中心发行
北京印刷二厂印制　02-J43-9643

Immediate lottery of the twelve Animal Signs, "Monkey drama", released by Chinese Welfare Lottery Center.

The people born in the Monkey year are consistent and righteous. They usually pay attention to details. They are the kind of person who holds the principle "Look not at what is contrary to propriety, listen not to what is contrary to propriety, speak not what is contrary to propriety". When they are not naughty, Monkey people are the nicest guys you have ever met. The problem is that Monkey people are the kind of childish. They like to do some monkey tricks just like children. Once Monkey people become mischievous, you must be careful.

Monkey people are always popular and irresistible even when they are over-conceited and long-winded. They can bring laughter to others. They are affluent in wisdom and have sweet appearances. Moreover, they are very kind-hearted, which means they can be long-term valuable friends, good neighbors and excellent employees. The people born in the Monkey year are righteous by nature. They would rather try their best to finish tasks than to sit idle and enjoy the fruits of others' work, thinking how to put their names on finished products. The ability of solving problems is the most appreciable quality of Monkey people. They seem to be able to solve any problems.

Roles in the novel "A Journey to the West" The Monkey King-Sun Wukong.

The people born in the Monkey year are good business people. They are good at negotiating and skillful in bringing up details to make their counterparts compromise. The people born in the Monkey year like sports and they usually keep fit. If they begin to gain weight or their perimeters of stomach are widening, they would immediately go on diet and have exercises to lose weight. The people born in the Monkey year are consistent and stable internally. No matter how crazily they act, you needn't worry that they are too indulgent.

13

5 属猴人命理财运
Fate and Wealth Luck of Monkey People

The people born in the Monkey year will enjoy a kind of extremely happy childhood. Their parents will take perfect and minute care of them. For Monkey people, their childhood days are so nice that everything is carefree.

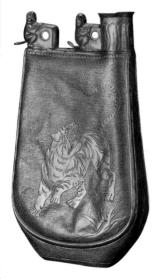

But there will be many problems once they become youths. Most of these problems are aroused because of their personalities. Usually Monkey people are active, thus they tend to cause troubles. Moreover, they have a kind of suspicious and oversensitive nature.

Generally speaking, Monkey people will enjoy peaceful lives in their late years. They will always feel lonely and indulge themselves into recollections of the past. It seems that they are seeking their childhoods that have already passed. Therefore, they are not very happy.

In general terms, their fortune luck is not bad. They are positive, extroverted and born to be optimists. On the whole, money won't be problems for them to worry about in their lives.

Besides, they are good at socializing and have broad interpersonal networks. Thus they usually get good opportunities to make money and get help from others.

Gold pot with monkey design, Liao (916-1125 AD).

Their warmhearted character is clearly reflected on the way they spend money. Sometimes they will splash about money unsparingly to satisfy their vanity.

For example when several friends are having dinner together, Monkey people are usually the ones to pay the bills. In fact, it is not necessary for one to puff himself up to his own cost. Isn't "go Dutch" good?

They also have another shortcoming: while they are doing one thing, they can be easily attracted by another new one, and then they will shift from the former to the latter. As a result, they can't wait for the benefits of anything they are doing, thus they will lose many opportunities.

Moreover, sometimes they do not think much of interpersonal relations. They will refuse others without thinking of others' pleadings. As a result, they will lose a lot of wealth fortune.

Generally speaking, Monkey people don't have the habit of saving money. When they have enough money on hand, they won't make full use of it. Instead, they will splash about money unrestrainedly. However, Monkey people will get unexpected money once they are old.

6 属猴人爱情婚姻
Love and Marriage of Monkey People

Monkey people are intelligent, smart, while argumentative and tricky. Therefore, they do not have good relationshisp with opposite sex and always quarrel with their spouses. However, they are passionate and fall in love easily. Because of half-hearted and changeful characters, they always dissatisfy and cannot gain true love. Though Monkey people are

Wild nature of Huangshan Mountain, by Shi Gufeng, 110cm x 69cm.

able to love others sincerely, their passion is cooled by their sharp insights and criticizing habits. Then their lovers will leave them unhesitatingly. Usually, females, born in the Monkey year, focus on males' appearances. They don't show friendship to males initiatively, but hope males could create romantic atmosphere to please them. When facing their husbands, they prefer to act as mature ladies at home. Therefore, they should learn how to do housework and show their consideration to their husbands. Besides, they need to teach their children with their husbands together.

Males born in the Monkey year have lots of girl friends

simultaneously and dislike loving one person with their whole hearts. If they are happy, they will treat their girl friends gently and thoughtfully. On the other hand, if they are angry, they hope others could leave them as far as possible. However, males born in the Monkey year pay great attention to affection actually. They often abandon themselves to love stories. They can even give up their jobs, wealth, and social positions for love. In their wives eyes, males born in the Monkey year are perfect lovers, but unsuccessful husbands. However, when gradually maturing into the middle age, they will change their way of thinking obviously. They would like to burden more responsibilities and do housework for their wives in the families.

Traditionally, it is appropriate for Monkey people to match Rat people or Dragon people. They are perfect pairs and enjoy happy lives. It is not appropriate for Monkey people to marry Tiger people or Pig people. Their marriages will be broken by unfitted personalities. If both of the two sides could be self-surrenders, the results of their marriage may be better.

Chinese Confucianism: Look not at what is contrary to propriety, listen not to what is contrary to propriety, speak not what is contrary to propriety.

7 属猴人工作事业
Careers of Monkey People

Monkey people can be called the kind of people with great wisdom and various abilities. Jobs that require unique conceptions and creativities are suitable for them. In this aspect, they can fulfill their potentials to the greatest extent.

The jobs with variations can better explore their potentials. As long as they have made perfect plans, together with the talented people all around them, Monkey people will surely achieve great successes.

Supposing there is a kind of job that requires people to devote themselves in their studies and do research and write all day long. They don't like time-consuming jobs.

Generally speaking, they would rather do unique things than ordinary ones. Compared with jobs that require doing routine affairs, free occupations are more suitable for Monkey people. They are also genius in starting up businesses. For example, jobs such as painters, decorators, and actors are fundamentally suitable for them.

Besides, in the aspects of politics and economy, they cannot only apply their initiatives and intelligence, but also their special social skills. They have peculiar gifts for art, culture, academy, science, and so on.

If they can apply their energetic spirits of service into businesses such as restaurant or cafe, Monkey people will be quite employable. The day when their businesses are

Feng-Shui mascot monkey for success.

Chinese Confucianism: Look not at what is contrary to propriety, listen not to what is contrary to propriety, speak not what is contrary to propriety.

prosperous will come in time.

Moreover, Monkey people are quite sensitive to the prevalent trend. For Monkey people who usually pursue changes, it is very suitable to undertake glorious rag trade. They will collect the latest information and know about the current fashion quickly. In order to purchase new products, they will search through the whole country and even foreign countries. But this occupation demands great patience. In this sense, it is hard for Monkey people to be designers. Unexpectedly, with their intelligence, super sensitivity, and foresight, Monkey people may become super top-grade designers or men of the time in relative industry if they cooperate with those who are stable and steadfast, with a diligent spirit.

Ancestor of human beings - monkey

Based on archaeological research, the ancestors of Primates, including human beings, are animals inhabiting on trees about 65 millions of years ago. Gradually, these animals evolved into original monkey about 25 millions of years ago. And about 15 millions years ago, one branch of the original monkey naturally evolved into modern monkey, and the other branch adapted itself to changing environments and evolved into human beings step by step.

8 属猴人五行生肖
Specification of the Five Elements for Monkey People

(1) 120 年五行属性编年历
The List of the Five Elements During a Period of 120 Years in the Gregorian Calendar

This section introduces in detail about which years and months, during a period of 120 years in the Gregorian calendar, constitute the Monkey year, and which one of the Five Elements is for each specific Monkey year.

Feb. 6th, 1932 to Jan. 25th, 1933 is the Metal Monkey year.
Jan. 25th, 1944 to Feb. 12th, 1945 is the Water Monkey year.
Feb. 12th, 1956 to Jan. 30th, 1957 is the Fire Monkey year.
Jan. 30th, 1968 to Feb. 16th, 1969 is the Earth Monkey year.
Feb. 16th, 1980 to Feb. 4th, 1981 is the Wood Monkey year.
Feb. 4th, 1992 to Jan. 22nd, 1993 is the Metal Monkey year.
Jan. 22nd, 2004 to Feb. 8th, 2005 is the Water Monkey year.
Feb. 8th, 2016 to Feb. 27th, 2017 is the Fire Monkey year.
Jan. 27th, 2028 to Feb. 12th, 2029 is the Earth Monkey year.
Feb. 12th, 2040 to Jan. 31st, 2041 is the Wood Monkey year.

The golden monkey bringing good luck.

Longevity.

（2）五行属性特征
Specification of the Five Elements for Monkey People

1. 土猴
People born in the Earth Monkey Year

From Jan. 30th, 1968 to Feb. 16th, 1969 and Jan. 27th, 2028 to Feb. 12th, 2029 is the Earth Monkey year.

Personalities of Earth Monkey People

Earth Monkey people are optimistic, frank, and persevering. Because seldom getting help from their brothers, they must establish businesses from nothing by themselves. They live hard lives in youth-hood. Until having mastered skills, they cannot succeed. After middle age, they will enjoy comfortable lives. Females born in the Earth Monkey year are a little bit stubborn. And it is good for them to marry at mature age, which can relieve displeasing conflicts after marriages.

Careers of Earth Monkey People

Feng-Shui mascot of Monkey people.

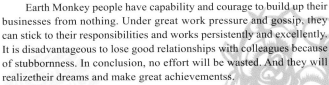

Earth Monkey people have capability and courage to build up their businesses from nothing. Under great work pressure and gossip, they can stick to their responsibilities and works persistently and excellently. It is disadvantageous to lose good relationships with colleagues because of stubbornness. In conclusion, no effort will be wasted. And they will realizetheir dreams and make great achievementss.

Health of Earth Monkey People

They should take good care of their health. Earth Monkey people have some bad habits. However, if they can pay attention to diets, have good rests, and have exercises regularly, they will be in good health.

Love of Earth Monkey People

Because of their personalities, males born in the Earth Monkey year are attractive to opposite sex. If encountering their favorite girls, Earth Monkey people should take actions to pursue their girls, and will achieve satisfied result. However, females born in the Earth Monkey year are likely to have fluctuating affection with many troubles. Therefore, the

females should hold relaxed attitudes toward affections. It is important to avoid making mountains out of molehills, which will hurt their lovers.

Wealth of Earth Monkey People

Earth Monkey people are lucky in wealth and gain a little bit unexpected wealth. Unfortunately, the money comes and goes quickly. However, when in financial problems, they will gain some money to go through the difficulties.

2. 金猴
People Born in the Metal Monkey Year

From Feb. 6th, 1932 to Jan. 25th, 1933 and from Feb. 4th, 1992 to Jan. 22nd 1993 is the Metal Monkey year.

Personalities of Metal Monkey People

Metal Monkey people are smart and eloquent, but impatient and stubborn. With self-confidence, they are able to establish their own businesses. Besides, they are playful, self-styled, and cunning. Therefore, it is possible for them to make mistakes because of self-styled smartness. As always playing tricks on others, they have bad relationships with others. They should avoid frivolity and fickleness, making themselves popular in others. It is of great help to their career development. As to family affairs, Metal Monkey people seldom get help or support from their brothers. They have to earn their own livings and build up their businesses from nothing. Both males and females born in the Metal Monkey year are better to marry at mature age. Otherwise, their marriages will be unlucky.

Careers of Metal Monkey People

Metal Monkey people do everything with facility. With the cooperation of favorable climate, good geographical environments, and others' support, they will become eminent. However, they do not have good relationships with others. It must be improved. Especially, they should not treat their colleagues and subordinates with strong arm. Otherwise, they will offend others and face more challenges when in higher positions. If they could

Marquis bringing in wealth.

improve their relationships with others, there would be more opportunities coming one after another. And then, it is the time to establish their own businesses or change their careers. Young people born in the Metal Monkey year need to study hard. Then they can make further progress. However, they often dispute with their classmates and friends. To avoid quarrels, they must have more tolerance.

Health of Metal Monkey People

As to health, Metal Monkey people are weak in immunity and apt to become ill. Therefore, they must pay attention to dietetic sanitation, especially avoiding food poisoning or calenture in summer.

Love of Metal Monkey People

Metal Monkey people don't know knacks of how to get along well with others. They should not trust others too readily. Besides, they should avoid being cheated by their best friends. There are full of frustrations on their way of pursuing love. Because of paramours' intervention, they become hesitated to choose between their beloved and the paramours, between trustful affections and aberrant ones. As a result, all the three sides will be hurt.

Wealth of Metal Monkey People

The knack of Metal Monkey people to become rich is to effectively manage capital amassment and cash flow. They earn money by hard working. Therefore, they should invest in real estates for inflation-proof, rather than spend money at will.

Eupatrid, by Wang Gengxin, 134cm x 67cm.

25

3. 水猴

People Born in the Water Monkey Year

From Jan. 25th, 1944 to Feb. 12th,1945 and from Jan. 22nd, 2004 to Feb. 8th, 2005 is the Water Monkey year.

Personalities of Water Monkey People

Water Monkey people are smart, dexterous, and ostentatious. They are inherent leaders with strong managerial ability. However, sometimes they make showy displays of their abilities, which gives others the aggressive impression and arouse disgusting feelings among others. It is disadvantageous to their careers development. Therefore, Earth Monkey people need to be self-restrained and try their best to improve their relationships with others. Furthermore, they should read more books to enrich themselves, which will also improve their luck. If they can fulfill all their potential, they will succeed undoubtedly. Both males and females born in the Earth Monkey year are lucky in love affairs. Because they are attractive to opposite sex, they can easily get help from opposite sex. Their spouses and they will have harmonic lives after marriage.

Careers of Water Monkey People

Water Monkey people somewhat fluctuate in the luck of wealth. They should have mental preparation in advance. In the right position, they are competent to finish their work with ease. As a result, their performances will become more understanding. When cooperating with comparative colleagues, they will feel with might redoubled. Under heavy workload, they should choose scientific and effective methods to improve their productivities.

Health of Water Monkey People

When always feeling physical weaknesses, necks' discomfort, dizziness, and headache, Water Monkey people should pay attention to diets. If feeling pain in throats, they must go to see doctors as soon as possible.

Love of Water Monkey People

Water Monkey people are spoiled by their parents. Their parents offer them their favorite toys and indulge them by every means. In their later years, they will get their children's filial piety. Their children always live together with them, and never make them feel lonely. They will enjoy happy lives in old age.

Feng-Shui mascot monkey for happiness.

Wealth of Water Monkey People

Because the Wealth Star shine over their head, Water Monkey people are lucky in wealth. They have opportunities to earn unexpected fortune. However, they should not depend on such unexpected wealth, and avoid getting into the increasing interests of gambling. If using wealth ineffectively, they will earn nothing in spite of their good luck.

4. 木猴

People Born in the Wood Monkey Year

From Feb. 16th, 1980 to Feb. 4th,1981 and from Feb. 12th, 2040 to Jan. 31st, 2041 is the Wood Monkey year.

Personalities of Wood Monkey People

Wood Monkey people are energetic, sympathetic, and punctual, with warm hearts to help others. As to work, they have strong responsibility and try their best to complete every task. However, because lacking self-confidence, they need support and encouragement from their relatives and friends. Though females born in the Wood Monkey year have bad-tempered husbands, their husbands have good relationshisp with them and treat them with warmth and caution. Their children show filial respect to them too. Therefore, females born in the Wood Monkey year have happy families. Their luck is smooth in old age.

Careers of Wood Monkey People

Wood Monkey people are lucky in career. Though under heavy workload and great pressure, they can solve problems successfully with their own abilities and earn excellent marks, winning their superiors' appreciation. Then, they have promotion opportunities. Wood Monkey people are hardworking guys. They always forget food and sleep in labs, in order to achieve a conclusion. Because of such attitude, they will make

Feng-Shui mascot monkey for longevity.

great progress in career.

Health of Wood Monkey People

Wood Monkey people should pay attention to the following aspects to keep health. When eating outside, they should pay attention to cleanness and sanitation in case of food poisoning. When enjoying outdoor activities, they should avoid exposing themselves to sunlight too long, otherwise they may get calenture. Avoid having wrong medicines. and working too hard.

Love of Wood Monkey People

Wood Monkey people have enviable luck in love affairs. Wood Monkey people, especially females, are good match to their spouses. Wood Monkey people are passionate, sober, and somewhat conservative. They and their spouses seldom quarrel with each other angrily. Though there are some small arguments in their family lives, they will reconcile with each other soon, as if nothing happened before.

Wealth of Wood Monkey People

Wood Monkey people are relatively busy and always travel a lot. They reap what they sow, thus achieving much. When making some money, they should invest in real estates and extend their businesses later, rather than spend carelessly.

5. 火猴
People Born in the Fire Monkey Year

Feng-Shui mascot monkey for success.

From Feb. 12th, 1956 to Jan. 30th, 1957 and from Feb. 8th, 2016 to Jan. 27th, 2017 is the Fire Monkey year.

Personalities of Fire Monkey People

Fire Monkey people advocate friendships, and have long-term goals, with business minds. However, they are impatient, adventurous, cynical, and unrealistic. So their lives are fluctuated. It is good for them to develop their careers outside their native places. In suchway, they will make great achievements. Males born in the Fire Monkey year will get help from their wives and have happy families.

Careers of Fire Monkey People

Fire Monkey people are persevering and courageous in pursuing their career goals. Their luck is steady and gradually advanced. Though workload is somewhat too heavy, they can handle it, with their own efforts. Then, they will get praises and appreciation from their superiors and colleagues. Therefore, they have promotion opportunities. Besides,

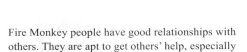

Fire Monkey people have good relationships with others. They are apt to get others' help, especially male elderships' guide and supports.

Health of Fire Monkey People

If in good health, Fire Monkey people are apt to drink and have drugs to stimulate themselves. They should try their best to keep away from these stimuli rather than abandon themselves. Besides, they need to pay attention to gastroenteritis.

Love of Fire Monkey People

Fire Monkey people are attractive and have good relationships with others. They have lots of friends in different areas. However, they should control their emotions to avoid falling in love too early. To love wrong people will hurt both sides.

Wealth of Fire Monkey People

Fire Monkey people are lucky in wealth. They can earn and accumulate lots of money. Furthermore, they also have opportunities to win prizes in lotteries, but the speculative activities are not good to them. They should invest in estates, such as gold and jade wares, real estates, and good stocks, for inflation proof.

Feng-Shui mascot monkey for happiness.

31

9 属猴人与十二星座
Monkey People and the Twelve Constellations

十二星座表
List of the Twelve Constellations for Monkey People

Feng-Shui mascot monkey for good luck.

	Monkey/Aries people are born from 21st, Mar. to 20th, Apr. in the Monkey year.
	Monkey/Taurus people are born from 21st, Apr. to 21st, May in the Monkey year.
	Monkey/Gemini people are born from 22nd, May to 21st, Jun. in the Monkey year.
	Monkey/Cancer people are born from 22nd, Jun. to 23rd, Jul. in the Monkey year.
	Monkey/Leo people are born from 24th, Jul. to 23rd, Aug. in the Monkey year.
	Monkey/Virgo people are born from 24th, Aug. to 23rd, Sept. in the Monkey year.
	Monkey/Libra people are born from 24th, Sept. to 23rd, Oct. in the Monkey year.
	Monkey/Scorpio people are born from 24th, Oct. to 23rd, Nov. in the Monkey year.
	Monkey/Sagittarius people are born from 24th, Nov. to 21st, Dec. in the Monkey year.
	Monkey/Capricorn people are born from 22nd, Dec. to 20th, Jan. in the Monkey year.
	Monkey/Aquarius people are born from 21st, Jan. to 19th, Feb. in the Monkey year.
	Monkey/Pisces people are born from 20th, Feb. to 20th, Mar. in the Monkey year.

猴／白羊座 3月21日－4月20日

Monkey / Aries People Born from 21st, Mar. to 20th, Apr. in the Monkey Year

The Symbol of the Aries

The symbol of the Aries, made of the two horns on the head of a ram, symbolizes courage and perseverance.

Personalities of Monkey/Aries People

Monkey/Aries people are incomparable conversationists. Monkey/Aries people are the most frank and forthright people in people's lives. When separated from such people, we will find most memorable parts about them are the words they have said. Monkey/Aries people are famous for their bluff and frank-hearted speeches. Monkey/Aries people like talking high-sounding words, but sometimes they will also irritate others very much. Monkey/Aries people are smart, strongly sympathetic, and care for their beloved.

Aries people with the intelligence and wittiness of Monkey people are extremely fascinating. However, sometimes Money/Aries people are too talkative, which makes other people suffer so much as to ask them to shut up. Money/Aries people don't really value very much the commonly so-called "success". Money/Aries people are not the kind of people who will overpower others by all means to achieve successes. Contrarily, Money/Aries people will have excellent performances in the programs they chose for themselves. They won't be affected by social or economical surroundings. All Money/Aries people want is to strive for their own goals, which may just appear to be impractical in others' eyes.

Monkey/Aries people have keen insight. Looking around, Monkey/Aries people can distinguish people's true essences and see through

people's gassing or bullshit. Monkey/Aries people are quite independent. When they are alone, they will be engaged in brilliant thinking. Monkey/Aries people can immerge themselves in reading books, doing researches, and striving for high positions. The inborn characteristics of the Monkey/Aries people are patient, and always act without delay.

Love of Monkey/Aries People

The inborn characteristics of Monkey/Aries people enable them to maintain a kind of long time marital relationship in monogamy. Monkey/Aries people usually have spouses, but it doesn't mean they like staying at home, enjoying romantic evenings with their wonderful spouses. Instead, Monkey/Aries people like going out, chatting with everyone and getting responses from them. Monkey /Aries people are skillful in social communications. But little unfaithfulness won't reduce their sincere and long-term love toward their beloved; in fact, Monkey/Aries people are ardent and devoted lovers.

Careers of Monkey/Aries People

Monkey/Aries people may take up jobs that require simply laborious work. No matter what kinds of jobs they choose, they can make great achievements. Many Monkey/Aries people have their own businesses, for example, they may have their own companies or operate their own stores. Jobs that Monkey/Aries people favor include costume designing and manufacturing, psychology, teachers, medical care, and business.

猴 / 金牛座 4月21日—5月21日

Monkey / Taurus People Born from 21st, Apr. to 21st, May in the Monkey Year

The Symbol of the Taurus

The symbol of the Taurus, made of a circle and an arc, represents aspiration for material and spiritual life, as well as advantages of Taurus people in their lives.

Personalities of Monkey/Taurus People

Monkey people are good at guile and cheating. The characteristics of Taurus people can help to make busy and active Monkey people stable. The two kinds of characteristics make a lucky combination. One of the main characters of Monkey/Taurus people is that they are always in a steady status. Just like most people, Monkey/Taurus people can control their emotions. What is amazing about Monkey/Taurus people is that they seem to be even able to break away from traumas suddenly. Monkey/Taurus people can stay active even if they are in deep sorrow or being wailing loudly. Of course, Monkey/Taurus people will be the first ones who pull themselves away from sorrow soon and make plans for future. They are very practical and never indulge themselves in impractical dreams or unachievable desires. They are also very self-restrained and can make full use of time to finish their jobs. Balance and stability are important advantages of Monkey/Taurus people. When Monkey/Taurus people feel they get along with the world harmoniously, they will be very happy. Monkey/Taurus people rarely feel suspicious of themselves. They may feel panic in hearts sometimes, but hardly any chance can you see Monkey/Taurus people gaunt and blubbering out the bad situations they have felt. Monkey/Taurus people try their best to present with their

best sides to arouse others' confidence. Monkey/Taurus people are very kind-hearted. They often offer to take care of their friends who are ill. Despite they are generous in temperament, Monkey/Taurus people are embodiments of independence. They don't need companions when they go to movies or concerts, travel, or go dining or dancing, etc.

Love of Monkey/Taurus People

Different people have slightly different opinions on being faithful. For Monkey/Taurus people, being faithful to a relationship means loyalty, friendship and sincere love. Monkey/Taurus people's independence imposes threats to their emotional or marital relationships. For Monkey/Taurus people, love represents a rebirth of the two, and freedom. Monkey/Taurus people are always childish, fascinating, but seem unfathomable. Monkey/Taurus people are footloose. They always think they are in stable emotional relationships with others, but often the results turn out to be unpleasant.

Careers of Monkey/Taurus People

Monkey/Taurus people like spending money and know how to make money. They have kind and pleasant appearances and enjoy making friends. As a result, people like exchanging opinions with Monkey/Taurus people and learn their ways of getting with others. Appropriate jobs for Monkey/Taurus people include salespeople, public relation representatives, news reporters, and medicine people.

猴 / 双子座 5 月 22 日 -6 月 21 日
Monkey / Gemini People Born from 22nd, May to 21st, Jun. in the Monkey Year

The Symbol of the Gemini

Made up of the twins, the symbol of the Gemini indicates that a person is integrated both in body and in mind, which exactly expresses dual personalities of Gemini people.

Personalities of Monkey/Gemini People

Monkey/Gemini people never stop moving, and are always energetic. People may even doubt about whether Monkey/Gemini people need sleep. Monkey/Gemini people like talking. They are eager to perform in front of others with such strong eagerness that they appear to make self-display. They enjoy entertaining others. They will be pleased when they see others having fun. Monkey/Gemini people are very intelligent and have very creative minds. Take horse racing for example, Monkey/Gemini people may come up with innovative ideas about horse racing causes even if they know nothing about horses. The ideas may come into their minds one day when they watch a horse racing competition, and then they will take actions with great interests. Monkey/Gemini people hate doing the same things using the same methods, so they spend a lot of time thinking about new projects. Monkey/Gemini people are snobbish. They are fond of significant and ingenious things with larger size and high quality. Monkey/Gemini people think owning these things can make others admire them. Monkey/Gemini people hope to own at least a sports car with high speed, an expensive dog of well-known brand, and a fashionable and suitable spouse. These are parts of their performances. For Monkey/Gemini people, life is a play. Monkey/Gemini people are quite independent and responsible. They can work diligently in their offices as well as do spring-cleanings alone. They know how to do several things simultaneously. Watching them working is like watching a magician doing tricks in the central stage of a circus.

Love of Monkey/Gemini People

Monkey/Gemini people are not ordinary lovers. They want persistent love and the other side's attentions focused on them. Because of Monkey/Gemini people's delicate charms, Monkey/Gemini people can always win the hearts of the people they chase. Monkey/Gemini people are good at dealing with conflicts. They prefer the emotional relationships to be as clear as day. Once established, the relationship must provide constant and endless joys and happiness to Monkey/Gemini people. Things won't go complicated if you fall in love with Monkey/Gemini people. As long as you can devote your whole life loving Monkey/Gemini people, helping them with all chores, you will win their love. Because the genius may be too busy puffing up the balloons for the parties, and forget to wash dishes.

Careers of Monkey/Gemini People

Monkey/Gemini people are able to solve sinuous conflicts and overcome difficulties in their lives. They are capable of doing many jobs, from cancer experts to film directors. Monkey/Gemini people can bring their potentials into full play through changes and innovations. No matter what jobs they do, the jobs must provide opportunities for them to create and form new ideas.

猴／巨蟹座 6月22日－7月23日
Monkey / Cancer People Born from 22nd, Jun. to 23rd, Jul. in the Monkey Year

The Symbol of the Cancer

The symbol of the Cancer looks like the shell of a crab, which in fact represents tolerance and self-sacrifice spirit of mothers, who are always ready to shield families and friends at any cost.

Personalities of Monkey/Cancer People

Just like all Monkey people, Monkey/Cancer people are good at solving problems. Facing complicated and confusing situations, they can remain calm, analyze the problems and find quick solutions. Monkey/Cancer people are cautious and considerate; in order to succeed, They are almost regardless of anything. The only thing that can stop them is emotional affairs. They are very crafty Monkey people, meanwhile they are very the possessive and sensitive Cancer people. Having a loving heart is both advantage and disadvantage for them. For example, if Monkey/Gemini people's families don't like to develop in cities while they like, they will agree with their families' choice. Once falling in love, Monkey/Gemini people will be passionate, crazy, and act out of their minds, incurable. No matter what jobs they do, Monkey/Cancer people are prudent about money. They will make investments in reliable businesses and consolidate their wealth step by step. They won't strive to become extremely rich. However, they can always earn money. Gradually, they will accumulate considerable wealth. Monkey/Cancer people have great talents in art. Whether being experts or scholars, they are hard-working and can make great achievements. Besides talents, they are the Monkey people kind with wittiness and flexibility.

Love of Monkey/Cancer People

Monkey/Cancer people always want to possess things firmly. They are often suspicious of their beloved. It is not that they don't know how to love; quite on the contrary, they are quite skillful in flattering their lovers. They can do anything you can name out such as inviting their lovers to travel, giving presents, and so on. If you want to be the spouses of the talented and sentimental Monkey/Cancer people, you must act according to their wills. You should show your loyalty by complaining constantly and showing disobedience as if you have been spoiled. Besides, you will win their respects, for their interests are mainly in thoughts and emotions instead of physical bodies.

Careers of Monkey/Cancer People

Monkey/Cancer people are endowed with all kinds of abilities. Monkey/Cancer people can take up jobs related to art such as artists and writers. They have interests in almost everything from ballet to playwright. Enthusiastic, resourceful, and having wills to power, Monkey/Cancer people will achieve successes through making plans for projects and overtime work in their professions. One of their weaknesses is they are too sensitive. They will hesitate to take necessary actions just when a cause is about to reach its peak. The jobs suitable for Monkey/Cancer people include painters, musicians, poets, doctors, layers, antique goods traders, news reporters, and advertising agents.

猴 / 狮子座 7月24日－8月23日

Monkey / Leo People Born from 24th, Jul. to 23rd, Aug. in the Monkey Year

The Symbol of the Leo

Lions are valorous but also have unknown weaknesses. The symbol, looking like the rolled-up tail of a lion, indicates innermost loneliness of Leo people.

Personalities of Monkey/Leo People

Noble and supernatural, Monkey/Leo people never stop exploring. Sensitive and objective, they are never fooled by others. They are models of men who are steady and courageous. In fact, Monkey/Leo people are more courageous when they have to protect others. They can't bear to see their beloved hurt or treated unfairly. Though Monkey/Leo people are not aggressive, they will be regardless of anything else when they have to protect their friends. Monkey/Leo people appreciate strength. They admire people who dare to challenge power. Even though they are not likely to undertake revolutions and end up in jail, they are backboned persons who hold their own believes firmly. Monkey/Leo people are very attractive.

They are tidily dressed but they dislike perfumes or cosmetics. They are optimistic about their lives. They have emotional changes but they won't be in bad mood for a long time. Monkey/Leo people avoid by all means shouting to others. They are curious about everything, especially the people they meet. Monkey/Leo people like digging into others' recesses and have many friends of different classes. But they seldom have life-long bosom friends. They are objective with others. Monkey/Leo people never idealize people they newly meet. Monkey/Leo people

are skillful in surviving, but they don't like doing laborious work. They are not good at cleaning up, so their houses are always in a mess. Monkey/Leo people are interested in learning. New methods of solving problems can grasp their imaginations. They like solving problems and conflicts, most important, they like their beloved ones happy with big smile on their faces.

Love of Monkey/Leo People

Monkey/Leo people are very possessive and jealous. They appear to like playing jokes and being surrounded by others. Once falling in love, Monkey/Leo people are absolute captives; their love will be so ardent that they can't remain self-restrained.

Careers of Monkey/Leo People

Monkey/Leo people like diving into philosophical problems as well as pursuing life joys. They are sometimes mischievous but they have a temperament of poets. However, Monkey/Leo people like applying their art abilities into practical lives. They are surefooted. The combination makes Monkey/Leo people capable of taking up many careers. Usually they like sports and try to stay in perfect conditions. Their flexibilities make them fit for many jobs from swimming couches to guides, or from writers to social workers or secretaries. They are capable of doing any jobs except for kitchen stuff. It will be suitable for Monkey/Leo people to work alone without others' instructions.

猴／处女座 8月24日－9月23日
Monkey / Virgo People Born from 24th, Aug. to 23rd, Sept. in the Monkey Year

The Symbol of the Virgo

Consisted of a wheatear in hands of the Saturn, the symbol of the Virgo represents memories of the past and dreams of the future.

Personalities of Monkey/Virgo People

Virgo people are intelligent while Monkey people are crafty. Virgo people are inborn conservative while Monkey people are extroverted and active. Male Monkey/Virgo people think they are princes and female Monkey/Virgo people think they are as elegant as nobles. However, Male Monkey/Virgo will live hard lives. From Male Monkey/Virgo's childhoods to adulthoods, they have to struggle to succeed. Virgo people like to be with important people that have great power, which make them feel safe. However, Monkey people don't pay much attention to personal relations unless it is of practical use. The combination of the two makes the people have a lust for power and are extremely anxious. They want to control others' lives. Monkey/Virgo people think they have observant eyes on people, so Male Monkey/Virgo like interfering in others' businesses. On the other hand, they are very kind-hearted and willing to help those unfortunate people. Male Monkey/Virgo people are very generous, and are even ready to open their purses to help others. The problem is that they want to get praise or even greasiness from others by doing these. In fact, Monkey/Virgo people are selfish individualists. Monkey/Virgo people are born to be acrid and overwhelming authorities; they are insatiable and hold tight of material comforts. Monkey/Virgo people are restrained to details usually. They want everything to be

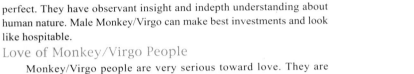

perfect. They have observant insight and indepth understanding about human nature. Male Monkey/Virgo can make best investments and look like hospitable.

Love of Monkey/Virgo People

Monkey/Virgo people are very serious toward love. They are extreme romanticists who will use every skill to court people of the opposite sex. The weakness of them is that they have to completely possess the one they love. If you fall in love with a Monkey/Virgo person, you should let him feel he is the only person in the world besides you.

Careers of Monkey/Virgo People

Monkey/Virgo people are good at dealing with trivial things. They go to work on time. Generally speaking, they will never ask for leave. They are not only practical, but also prudent and ambitious. Monkey/Virgo people will be good subordinates, but when they are bosses, they will never give up a tiny bit of power, nor will they let go chance that may make them famous. They hope to be well-known as soon as possible. Monkey/Virgo people are very strict with others. They value money and wealth very much. Appropriate jobs for Monkey/Virgo people includ charitarians, entrepreneurs and administrators.

45

猴／天秤座 9月24日－10月23日
Monkey / Libra People Born from 24th, Sept. to 23rd, Oct. in the Monkey Year

The Symbol of the Libra

The symbol of the Libra is a balanced scale, which indicates justness and balance.

Personalities of Monkey/Libra People

The ability and wisdom of Monkey/Libra people lie in the skillful ways they speak and write in business and art fields. Monkey/Libra people's fluent and prominent eloquence make them favored by their friends. Libra people tend to marry early because they are willing to live marriage lives. Monkey people are endowed with the ability to communicate skillfully with others. Monkey/Libra people don't like peaceful but boring lives. They consider the world a place for entertainment and are attracted to different activities. They like traveling around to experience and absorb novel and interesting things.

Monkey/Libra people are good at manipulating others and will lose no chance to do this. However, Monkey/Libra people are not parasites. In fact, Monkey/Libra people are very energetic and endowed with middle aptitude, appearing to be bright and witty.

Monkey/Libra people are lighthearted and cheerful in some way. They are sometimes as childish as children with flickering light in their eyes. They have very

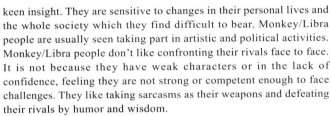

keen insight. They are sensitive to changes in their personal lives and the whole society which they find difficult to bear. Monkey/Libra people are usually seen taking part in artistic and political activities. Monkey/Libra people don't like confronting their rivals face to face. It is not because they have weak characters or in the lack of confidence, feeling they are not strong or competent enough to face challenges. They like taking sarcasms as their weapons and defeating their rivals by humor and wisdom.

Love of Monkey/Libra People

Monkey/Libra people value emotions very much. They pursue balance between the two sides in emotional or marital relationships. Monkey/Libra people hope the love between the two sides is ardent. To create nice marriage lives together, Monkey/Libra people want the two sides to be independent individuals that can offer strong support to each other. If Monkey/Libra people have obtained something from the other side, they will surely get return. If attracted by Monkey/Libra people, you can be sure the emotional relationships with them are just the lifelong happiness you are seeking for.

Careers of Monkey/Libra People

The ability and wisdom of Monkey/Libra people lie in how they use words to express their ideas. The best way of employing them is to let them write alone in offices or rush bout to sell things. Appropriate jobs for them include real estate agents, actors, professors, insurance agents, speechwriters, social workers, public relationship representatives.

猴 / 天蝎座 10 月 24 日 —11 月 23 日
Monkey / Scorpio People Born from 24th, Oct. to 23rd, Nov. in the Monkey Year

The Symbol of the Scorpio

A highly turned-up tail symbolizes inner aspiration of Scorpio people, and furthermore, indicates that their determination to fulfill their dreams won't change until their death.

Personalities of Monkey/Scorpio People

Monkey/Scorpio people have designing abilities and creativities. They can make great achievements. Monkey/Scorpio people have all the complicated traits of Scorpio people. They are up to all dodges and like unintelligible enigmas. Monkey/Scorpio people are sharp as well as strong. But they will pretend to be lively or childish to conceal their dark side of personalities. Monkey/Scorpio people are witty and lively. They are fond of freedom and changes. Moreover, they have the abilities to detour. No matter how great failures they have met, they will try to find suitable ways out. Basically, they are self-centered people, and hope to make achievements all by their own. Monkey people can lead others to successes, but they must first get rid of the atrocity of Scorpio people. Monkey/Scorpio people are highly creative. They can bring up complicated plans and finish them. Monkey people are mild and restrained, the characteristics of Scorpio people can help to rouse their aspirations and bring them into fields they have never been to. At first, Monkey/Scorpio people may hate and complain about new environments that they can't get accustomed to. But once they are engaged in it, they will immediately adapt to the new environment from which they wanted to escape before.

Monkey/Scorpio people are too talkative. An old disc seems to have been put in their brains. It replays again and again. Monkey/Scorpio people have to be reminded by others to stop talking too much. Fortunately, they face criticisms with laugh instead of getting angry.

Love of Monkey/Scorpio People

Monkey/Scorpio people are energetic lovers. They want to be praised so as to enjoy joyful and exciting atmospheres. They have no time to join in the fun on occasion, for their interests are in long time emotional relationships.

Careers of Monkey/Scorpio People

Monkey/Scorpio people have gifts for artistic creations, and they are also able to do translations. They are good story-tellers. They like talking, with the ability and wisdom of linking up stories. It is suitable for them to work in small groups. They pay great attention to their working achievements. When the deadline for work comes near, they will get irascible. They don't want to be bosses. They only hope to work in their most interested areas alone. Appropriate jobs for them include photographers, musicians, gardeners, pottery makers, dance designers, shipbuilders, sound managers, and historians.

猴 / 人马座 11 月 24 日 －12 月 21 日

Monkey / Sagittarius People Born from 24th, Nov. to 21st, Dec. in the Monkey Year

The Symbol of the Sagittarius

The symbol of the Sagittarius is made of a flying arrow, which represents the determination of Sagittarius people to pursue freedom, and also indicates their dreams.

Personalities of Monkey/Sagittarius People

Monkey/Sagittarius people are freethinkers. They are selfishless and cheerful. Differences between Monkey people and Sagittarius people are that Sagittarius people are altruists with naive characters and are not afraid of difficulties, while Monkey people don't. Monkey/Sagittarius people are craftier and try not to act too straightly. They are good at roundabout advancements. Monkey/Sagittarius people rarely challenge their rivals directly unless they are sure they will win. The combination of the two make Monkey/Sagittarius people inborn leaders. They have enough enthusiasms and strength to take up difficult causes with abilities of using guile and cheating. Monkey/Sagittarius people like being in charge of things. They like making decisions, instructing others, making laws, and drafting plans and innovations. Monkey/Sagittarius people think in the ways of organizers and consider things deeply into cores. Monkey/Sagittarius people are sincere, which makes them attractive and convincible. Monkey/Sagittarius people like talking in front of people or debate sharply on problems with broad knowledge. They like spending money and dislike being involved in insignificant things. Monkey/Sagittarius people are good at public relations and are very interested in wealth and power. Being ambassadors shows their best performances.

Monkey/Sagittarius people know how to divert others' opinions to their sides.

Love of Monkey/Sagittarius People

Monkey/Sagittarius people will feel uneasy in intimate relationships. They never love easily and tend to escape from the bondage of marriages. Monkey/Sagittarius people will be hesitant before they get married or live with others. Monkey/Sagittarius people will doubt if they will feel bored with their beloved in the first few years. Their characters deny any emotional responsibilities. If you would like to challenge Monkey/Sagittarius people, you'd better treat them the same way they treat you. Don't be captives easily, or Monkey/Sagittarius people will soon feel bored of you.

Careers of Monkey/Sagittarius People

Monkey/Sagittarius people rarely choose roads without difficulties or dangers. Monkey/Sagittarius people are good at managing and have gifts in organizing. They are problem-solving people. Of course, Monkey/Sagittarius people have the qualities of being leaders and are willing to be bosses. Appropriate jobs for them include politicians, writers, ambassadors, managers, and business men, etc.

猴 / 摩羯座 12 月 22 日 — 1 月 20 日

Monkey / Capricorn People Born from 22nd, Dec. to 20th, Jan. in the Monkey Year

The Symbol of the Capricorn

Made of horns of a goat and a tail of a fish, the symbol of the Capricorn indicates Capricorn people's adaptability and tolerance to environments.

Personalities of Monkey/Capricorn People

In appearance, Monkey/Capricorn people are not sensitive or nervous. Their sagacious manners and unique appearances show their confidence. They have exalted dispositions. Under their steady

appearances, suffering souls are concealed. Monkey/Capricorn people appear to be serious. In fact, unless you are very familiar with Monkey/Capricorn people, and have a deep knowledge of their lives, you won't be able to know the dark side of their characters. In front of others, Monkey/Capricorn people are respectable while at home they may be quite annoying. If you meet them in joyful atmospheres or at parties after sound drinking and eating, you will see performers with flicking eyes, in high spirits and full of jokes and stories. Monkey/Capricorn people can tell stories precisely with rich details and make them sound interesting. Monkey/Capricorn people appear to be smart and lively, full of wisdom. However,

On Jan. 25, 1992, China releaed stamps of the Money year. The designs include a picture of a monkey peach indicating longevity and a picture of pies on a plum's branches.

once they get home, the whole scene will be totally different. Monkey/Capricorn people think in their private lives, they must create a kind of order to take charge of the important things in their lives. They take the duties seriously. Where are daily necessities? Why supper is not ready yet? Why not clean the floor? What's wrong with your socks? Why don't think hard? In these occasions Monkey/Capricorn people like policepersons.

Love of Monkey/Capricorn People

In love, Monkey/Capricorn people value love quality rather than quantity. They'd rather love deeply forever for once. Their demand of love is quite strange. Usually they will choose one special person to share their secrets and live intimate lives together.

Careers of Monkey/Capricorn People

Pursuing goals in Monkey/Capricorn people careers is destination of lives. Monkey/Capricorn people are against laziness. They are creative and talented at explaining lives. Monkey/Capricorn people know how to express their opinions through stories. Appropriate jobs for them include film or drama directors, actors, singers, dancers, and writers, etc.

猴 / 宝瓶座 1 月 21 日 —2 月 19 日
Monkey / Aquarius People Born from 21st, Jan. to 19th, Feb. in the Monkey Year

The Symbol of the Aquarius

The symbol of the Aquarius is a stream of water pouring out from a bottle. It represents intellectuality and wisdom of Aquarius people, and furthermore, makes them the wisest ones in people of the twelve Constellations.

Personalities of Monkey/Aquarius People

Monkey/Aquarius people have broad knowledge and are deep thinkers. Monkey people's keen insight improves Aquarius people's knowledge about truth and keeps them live along with the reality. The combination is harmonious, and has potentials to develop. Monkey/Aquarius people are quite capable of language using. Words are the sharp tools of the prudential Monkey/Aquarius people. The sense of rebellion, or at least the high sensitiveness to certain social changes is revealed in every Monkey/Aquarius people's works. Not through power, but through works will Monkey/Aquarius people exert their power on others. Monkey/Aquarius people lead, instruct, or suggest other people, leading them advancing toward a better world. Monkey/Aquarius people are strong-willed and diligent. They hope to make achievements and usually they can get what they want. Moreover, they are versatile. A Monkey/Aquarius poet is not only able to write

poems, but can also design skyscrapers or feed an elephant from Africa. Monkey/Aquarius people are actionists. What they concern most is that their jobs are related to human development. They don't care about wealth or reputation. So long as they perform excellently in work, they will feel contented. To them, making achievements is most important in their lives.

Love of Monkey/Aquarius People

They fall in love without knowing. They need love and try to seek companions to share their worries and happiness. Monkey/Aquarius people tend to be unfaithful in love. But that is only for fun. They hope to get comforts and care form their beloved. Busy

and smart Monkey/Aquarius people like to make themselves beautiful, but they demand their companions more of inner beauty than outside appearances.

Careers of Monkey/Aquarius People

Monkey/Aquarius people are very independent; they can reasonably push their plans. Appropriate jobs for them include writers, directors, and actor, etc.

猴 / 双鱼座 2 月 20 日 –3 月 20 日
Monkey / Pisces People Born from 20th, Feb. to 20th, Mar. in the Monkey Year

The Symbol of the Pisces

Fishes in water symbolize dreams of Pisces people, while the two fish, tied down tightly by a thread, explicitly reveal Pisces people's complicate feelings to spirit and matters.

Personalities of Monkey/Pisces People

Monkey/Pisces people love beauty. They can usually get what they want. They are inborn to be gracious. People are proud of Monkey/Pisces people's elegant dressing and beautiful jewelries. Monkey/Pisces people are opportunists who spend their whole lives on busy calculating. Monkey/Pisces people have creative insights. They change their minds very quickly. They decide to love or hate somebody considering the benefits they can get from that person. Monkey/Pisces people hold Peripateticism as their philosophy. They are apt to take extreme actions. They may have health problems such as drinking or eating too much. However, Monkey people are not self-destroyers. Monkey/Pisces people know when to stop indulgence and go back to their regular lives. They know how to win others' friendships and hold it tightly in hands. Monkey/Pisces people treat friendships as precious as love and value it very much. Characteristics of Pisces

people are combined with the sharpness of Monkey people to form a characteristic that appears to be smooth. Monkey/Pisces people generally hold the attitude that "basically I trust others, but once I was hurt, I will strike back regardlessly." Monkey/Pisces people will never feel guilty even if they hit back severely.

Love of Monkey/Pisces People

Monkey/Pisces people will experience a lot in their love affairs. They are not only attractive, but also very fascinating and mysterious. Monkey/Pisces people have a sense of self-satisfaction and are glad to be the focuses of others' attention.

Careers of Monkey/Pisces People

Monkey/Pisces people are quite versatile in abilities. They are always quite healthy. But because of the unchangeable living styles, incidents may happen sometimes. Monkey/Pisces people's acute brains can follow the world's pace. They have gifts for wring and interpreting. Appropriate jobs for them include politicians, insurance salespeople, military men, and actors, etc.

10 属猴人生时吉凶
Fate of Monkey People Born in Different Hours

Born in "*Zi* hour" (11:00 p.m.-1:00 a.m.)

The Monkey people born "*Zi* hour" will have good luck in their careers and wealth. They were endowed by the God with leadership. They will be confronted with barriers casually and the decline in their intelligence. In this period, they should keep a kind of disimpassioned attitude toward gossips around them, and then they will be in good luck. The Monkey people born in "*Zi* hour" will meet their crucial year at the age of 49, and pass away at the age of 87.

Born in "*Chou* hour" (1:00 a.m.-3:00 a.m.)

The Monkey people born in "*Chou* hour" will live smooth lives and have good luck in wealth and reputations. They will have both the God and goblin in their lives, so the good luck and the bad luck of the Monkey people will be in counterbalance. Generally, they will turn all ill luck into good. The Monkey people born in "*Chou* hour" will meet their crucial years at the age of 23 and 46, and pass away at the age of 81.

Born in "*Yin* hour" (3:00 a.m.-5:00 a.m.)

The Monkey people born in "*Yin* hour" will work hard and live rough lives in their youth-hood. The Monkey people born in this period will be defeated in their careers and have extremely bad luck in their 17 years' old, then will become lucky in 40, and meet notable people in their late years. For the Monkey people born in the early period of "*Yin* hour",

Invested with marquis.

they will be clever and have good luck in wealth. For Monkey people born in the middle period of "*Yin* hour", they will turn to better luck after their 40 years' age. The Monkey people born in "*Yin* hour" will meet their crucial year at the age of 49, and pass away at the age of 76.

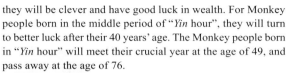

Born in "*Mao* hour" (5:00 a.m.-7:00 a.m.)

The Monkey people born in "*Mao* hour" will have good luck and needn't work too hard. They cannot depend too much on their parents or brothers. For the Monkey people born in the early period of "*Mao* hour", they will not be incompatible with their mothers, and have an only half start in their studies. For the Monkey people born in the middle period of "*Mao* hour", male ones will be in power and female ones will have good luck. For the Monkey people born in the late period of "*Mao* hour", they will be incompatible with their fathers, and their children would not have great achievements. The Monkey people born in "*Mao* hour" will meet their crucial year at the age of 55, and pass away at the age of 78.

Born in "*Chen* hour" (7:00 a.m.-9:00 a.m.)

The Monkey people born in "*Chen* hour" will be clever, determined, and healthy, and have good luck in their middle age and late years. Female Monkey people will live lonely lives and are quite confident, and they should establish better relationships with others. The Monkey people born in this period will have healthy parents and dependable relatives. They are kind-hearted and impartial. They will have both good luck and good wealth fortune, and establish their families away off their ancestors.

Born in "*Si* hour" (9:00 a.m.-11:00 a.m.)

The Monkey people born in "*Si* hour" will have outstanding intelligence. They will not have good predestined relationships with their families, and will establish their families away off their ancestors. The female Monkey people born in this period are peacockish and addicted to alcoholic. It will be difficult for them to have good marriages. The Monkey

people born in "*Si* hour" cannot depend too much on their brothers and don't have close relationships with their relatives. They are not expected to marry too early. They will have successes and failures alternatively, but they will have good wealth luck in their late years. Machining industry is suitable for the Monkey people. They should be careful at the age of 31, and will pass away at the age of 84.

Born in "*Wu* hour" (11:00 a.m.-1:00 p.m.)

The Monkey people born in "*Wu* hour" will be quite clever, but they cannot hold their ancestors' properties. The Female Monkey people are fascinating and extravagant. The Monkey people born in this period will have good luck to meet notable people, and can depend on brothers. They will have ordinary luck. They will have better luck after 30. They will live tough lives first and smooth lives in late years. Careers such as doctor and nurse are suitable for them. The Monkey people born in "*Mao* hour" will meet their crucial years at the age of 32 and 45, and pass away at the age of 85.

Born in "*Wei* hour" (1:00 p.m.-3:00 p.m.)

The Monkey people born in "*Wei* hour" cannot depend on their parents or brothers. They will be incompatible with their wives and children. The Female Monkey people born in this period are intelligent and have good luck in their careers. They always enjoy changes, and they can keep their families well, and support their husbands. The Monkey people will have good relationships with their brothers, but will be incompatible with their first wives. They should be careful at the age of 56, and will pass away at the age of 85.

Born in "*Shen* hour" (3:00 p.m.-5:00 p.m.)

The Monkey people born in this period will live harmonious lives in their marriages, and they should hold their behaviors and emotions well because of the fluctuations in their mood, otherwise, they will fail in their marriages. They are incompatible with their fathers, and have bad relationships with their brothers or relatives. They are clever, and can meet notable people. They will live tough lives in their early years. They will live smooth lives in their 30 years' age, and have good luck in their 40. They should be careful at the age of

42, and will pass away at the age of 79.

Born in "*You* hour" (5:00 p.m.-7:00 p.m.)

The Monkey people born in this period will live tough lives in their childhood, and will be separated from their brothers. The Male Monkey people are easily to be brought up; while the Female Monkey people are emotional, arrogant, and are good at keeping secrets. They will be likely to be in power, and meet their notable people easily. They cannot depend on their brothers, and live away from their brothers as well. The Female Monkey people are dissolute, thus they should be aware about their behaviors. The careers suitable for the Monkey people born in this period are teachers or art and literature. They should be careful at the age of 49 and 78.

Born in "*Xu* hour" (7:00 p.m.-9:00 p.m.)

The Monkey people born in this period are fascinating, and strive for their lives independently, and will have good wealth fortune. Female Monkey people are peacockish, and hot-tempered, and they are impatient, and are indifferent to money. The Monkey people born in this period will be power, but they cannot depend on their relatives. They are impatient, kind-hearted and knowledgeable, and have good marriages. The careers suitable for them are in agriculture field or speculation. The Monkey people born in "*Xu* hour" will meet their crucial year at the age of 55, and pass away at the age of 84.

Born in "*Hai* hour" (9:00 p.m.-11:00 p.m.)

The Monkey people born in this period are not skillful in interpersonal communications, but are good at handicrafts. The Female Monkey people are upright, hot-tempered that will be quickly dispelled, and will have good wealth fortune. The Monkey people born in this hour will have good luck, but cannot depend on their relatives, and will live tough lives in their years. They are clement, but do not have loose relationships with their brothers. The Male Monkey people will marry two wives, and the female Monkey people will be incompatible with their husbands. Art is their suitable career. The Monkey people born in "*Hai* hour" should be careful at the age of 49, and will pass away at the age of 78.

11 属猴人十二年流年运程
Fate of Monkey People in the Twelve Animal Years

Monkey people are versatile. They will distinguish themselves from others in youth-hood. Generally speaking, they have good luck in all their lives. It is their advantages to set further goals and strive to realize these goals, never feeling satisfied with small achievements. However, their impatience or arrogance will disgust others, resulting failures probably.

In Sept. 30th, 2000, Macao released a set of stamps, "Literature and characters - A Journey to the West".

文學與人物－西遊記
Literatura e Personagens Literárias - Jornada para Ocidente

0650094

On Dec. 1, 1979, China released the first set of stamps whose content comes from Chinese classical literature "A Journey to the West". In the novel, the personalized god of monkey, Sun Wukong, is a wise, courageous, and powerful hero.

属猴人遇鼠年的流年运程
Fate of Monkey People in the Rat Year

Feng-Shui mascot rat for money.

In the Rat year, Monkey people will be in good luck in general, but in ups-and-downs in some insignificant aspects. For the Monkey people who are born to be arrogant and aggressive, their luck will experience a great turnaround in the Rat year.

In the Rat year, Monkey people will have good wealth luck and they will gain more power. The Monkey people who are bosses will recruit excellent subordinates. And the Monkey people who are employees will be appreciated by their supervisors. In the year, Monkey people will have good luck to give good account of themselves. And there is more good news for them than bad news. However, they should handle household affairs carefully.

In the aspects of career and wealth, the Monkey people born in 1944 will have different luck in the Rat year. The changes could bring benefits to Monkey people in long-term, but have negative effects in short-term. Thus, the Monkey people should open their minds. For them, good wealth luck is out of question, while their power will be eclipsed in the year. The Monkey people born in years other than 1944 will have good opportunities to get promoted to senior management, blessed by the auspicious star, *jiangxing*. Moreover, with auspicious stars including *santai* and *jinkui* shinning on their heads, these Monkey people will have good wealth luck. In the Rat year, it is no doubt that Monkey people will make money in distant places, but they won't get profits from speculative investments. Blessed by the auspicious star, *yima*, Monkey people will have increased opportunities in foreign lands and get help from overseas notable persons. And they will face many changes such as moving houses, changing jobs, or migrating. In the Rat year, Monkey people will have up-and-down career luck. Depressed by arguments in officialdom, Monkey people will hardly remain good relationships with others.

属猴人遇牛年的流年运程
Fate of Monkey People in the Ox Year

Feng-Shui mascot ox for longevity.

In the Ox year, Monkey people will turn over a new leaf and become more graceful. Monkey people already have good luck of power and wealth. Upon Ox year, Monkey people will have babies born into their families and have good opportunities to make money. And their career development will be successful in the year. But it is a little bit regrettable that there will appear an ominous star, *liuxia,* which will negatively influence health of female Monkey people, and bring bad luck to male ones in distant places and disturb their minds. In general, Monkey people should strengthen old friendships and give good account of themselves. They will achieve much in the Ox year. Additionally, their trenchant manners will be improved in the year.

In the Ox year, Monkey people will have good luck to make investments and give good account of themselves in the third and 11th months of the year. Moreover, with the auspicious star, *tianxi,* shinning on their heads, monkey people will be very happy, and they should do more charitable deeds and attend more social activities. The Monkey people born in 1944 or 1968 will have the best luck among all Monkey people to get promoted or start up new businesses. Especially, those born in 1944 will become energetic and make accomplishments undoubtedly. The Monkey people born in 1956 should try their best to give good account of themselves. And the Monkey people born in 1932 or 1980 will have a smooth, placid, but rich and colorful Ox year. Monkey people will have the best luck to purchase houses in the third, sixth, ninth, and 12th months of the year. It is necessary for Monkey people to hold birthday parties in the year. They could go through any trouble by keeping cautious.

属猴人遇虎年的流年运程
Fate of Monkey People in the Tiger Year

Feng-Shui mascot tiger for exorcising evils.

In the Tiger year, Monkey people will face great changes when making investments. However, if they could handle the situation with great care, they would create good opportunities out of risks, and make their luck better.

If they had enhanced luck in the Ox year, they should become more cautious in the Tiger year. If they had bad luck in the Ox year, Monkey people will change themselves completely different and face many new chances in the Tiger. In the year, female Monkey people will have better luck than male ones. Female Monkey people will become aglow with health, while male ones might run into troubles when making investments. Especially, they should guard against troubles brought by their partners.

In the Tiger year, there will appear the auspicious star, *yima*, which indicates that Monkey people will face many changes such as traveling, changing jobs, moving houses, and falling sick. They will experience a critical difficulty in their lives. But fortunately, they will become more sophisticated and open-minded in the year.

In the aspects of career and wealth, Monkey people should remain conservative. However, it is often found that Monkey people are aggressive and run into dangers. In the year, Monkey people's wealth luck is in great ups-and-downs. The Monkey people born in 1944 or 1980 will have the best luck among all Monkey people, and they could go through the *taisui* year successfully. The Monkey people born in 1956 will gain authority and fame with eloquence. And the Monkey people born in 1968 will have good luck only in areas of literature and art.

属猴人遇兔年的流年运程
Fate of Monkey People in the Rabbit Year

In the Tiger year, there will appear lots of troubles in Monkey people's families, which make Monkey people annoyed very much. Moreover, their family members might be in bad health, while there's nothing good or unusual to report in their affectional lives. In the Tiger year, they have given vent to their complaints restrained for many years. Experiencing many changes and difficulties, Monkey people have become more sophisticated and mature. Upon the Rabbit year, everything goes well and smoothly and Monkey people will have good luck to purchase houses or start up new businesses. Additionally, the auspicious star, *dixie,* could dissolve any bad luck brought by ominous stars including *tiansha, liuhai, langan, baobai,* and *tiane.*

Feng-Shui mascot rabbit for harmony.

In the Rabbit year, the Monkey people born in 1956 will be blessed by the auspicious star, *tianyi,* and have good luck to invest in real estate. And the Monkey people born in 1920, 1944, or 1980 should denote blood to dissolve bad luck. The Monkey people born in 1944 will be in up-and-down wealth luck. They should open their minds to others' opinions rather than keep opinionated. Moreover, they should avoid argue with notable persons who could help them a lot. Blessed by the auspicious star, *jinyao,* the Monkey people born in 1968 should make full use their good opportunities to get further education and enhance friendships, never abandon themselves in adversities. And the Monkey people born in 1980 will have relative worse luck in the Rabbit year. Monkey people will have the best wealth luck in the second, fourth, and 11th months of the Rabbit year. Generally speaking, Monkey people will keep their minds and bodies busy and work hard. It is a good year for them to make further progress, compensating for their wasted time and energy in the last year.

属猴人遇龙年的流年运程
Fate of Monkey People in the Dragon Year

In the Dragon year, Monkey people have been recovering from illnesses for two years. There will appear the auspicious star, *huagai,* which could bring good luck of career and reputation to Monkey people. Additionally, male Monkey people will have better luck than female ones. Monkey people's luck in the Dragon year is acceptable but not as good as their luck in the Snake year. So they should remain careful and steady in the Dragon year.

Monkey people will feel restrained in many aspects, and can't bring their abilities into full play. Thus, in the Dragon year, Monkey people should cooperate with Snake people, Rat people, or Dragon people.

In the third month of the Dragon year, Monkey people will have good luck of career and wealth. Male Monkey people, especially those working in areas of art, politics, or education, will gain increased fame, as well as recognitions and appreciations. With the auspicious star, *huagai,* shinning on their heads, Monkey people will have good career luck but bad marriage luck in the Dragon year.

The Monkey people born in 1956 will have good luck to gain both lots of expected and unexpected wealth. The Monkey people born in 1944 will gain more fame than benefits, and they will be very busy. The Monkey people born in 1968 will get promoted through their excellent performances and hard working. And the Monkey people born in 1980 will make progress, and become the focus of public attentions. But they should be careful in case that they would be involved into arguments or other troubles, and that their psychosis would influence their grades significantly. In the Dragon year, Monkey people should give good account of themselves, though they might not succeed in every aspect. In the year, they should make friends extensively and avoid biting off more than they can chew.

Feng-Shui mascot dragon for promotion.

属猴人遇蛇年的流年运程
Fate of Monkey People in the Snake Year

Feng-Shui mascot snake for peace.

In recent years, Monkey people's lives seem boring and they often feel unhappy and unsatisfied to their current smooth and peaceful lives. Upon the Snake year, Monkey people will feel excited. There will appear many auspicious stars as well as notable persons who can help Monkey people a lot. With these good opportunities, Monkey people could turn ill luck into good, and their careers will enter into a new stage. In the aspect of career, Monkey people should try their best and give good account of themselves. They could make many breakthroughs in the Snake year.

Monkey people will have the best wealth luck in 11th month of the year, and not bad luck in the other months, except third and seventh months in which they are liable to waste some money. Generally speaking, in the Snake year, everything goes well as Monkey people wish.

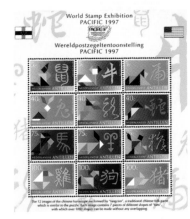

World Stamp Exhibition
PACIFIC 1997

Wereldpostzegeltentoonstelling
PACIFIC 1997

The 12 images of the chinese horoscope are formed by "tangram", a traditional chinese folk game which is similar to the puzzle. Each image contains 7 pieces of different shapes of "tans" with which over 1000 shapes can be made without any overlapping.

Antilles in North America is the Netherlandish colonial in the West Indies. It has released stamps of the twelve Animal Signs since 1997.

69

属猴人遇马年的流年运程
Fate of Monkey People in the Horse Year

Feng-Shui mascot horse for wealth.

Having been working hard for two years, Monkey people will become closer to their long-term goals. Out of painstaking work comes peaceful time. In the Horse year, Monkey people will still have good luck to make much money. Generally speaking, Monkey people's luck in the Horse year is not as good as that in previous two years. But the Monkey people born in 1944 or 1968 will have very good wealth luck, while the Monkey people born in 1932 will be in bad health.

Monkey people will have good wealth luck in the fourth, eighth, and 11th months of the Horse year. Especially, in the 11th month, they could make lots of money. But Monkey people should be careful not to spend too much money in the first month. The amount of money they spend in the first month will greatly influence their career development.

The Monkey people born in 1956 will make progress in career. Additionally, they will have good opportunities to travel a lot. But they will also feel homesick and could not enjoy their trips as much as they wish. In the Horse year, Monkey people should be careful since they are liable to be involved into arguments. In the year, since they are arrogant and aggressive, Monkey people will offend others by careless words. Moreover, they will experience adventures in the third month of the year, and get lots of unexpected wealth. It is difficult to say the experience indicates good or bad luck. In the year, Monkey people should do more charitable deeds, cultivating their moral characters in order to have a successful year.

属猴人遇羊年的流年运程
Fate of Monkey People in the Goat Year

In the Goat year, Monkey people will make little money. And they have to wait for good opportunities to gain more. If they took risks to go their own way, the more they invest, the greater failures they would experience. Therefore, Monkey people should spend more time on study and rest, conserving strength for future challenges and success.

In the Goat year, Monkey people will have ordinary luck. Whenever they make progress, they would also be involved into troubles. If they went on striving hard, they could certainly make some accomplishments. However, they will get half the result with twice the effort, compared with their good luck two or three years

Feng-Shui mascot goat for good salaries.

ago. In the year, Monkey people will be in good or bad health, while their family lives are not harmonious as they wish. Moreover, their arrogance might make them more opinionated, and their words trenchant words might hurt their friends or colleagues. It is hard for Monkey people to get help of notable persons in the Goat year. Thus, Monkey people should be carefully guard against being circumvented or involved into unnecessary arguments.

Monkey year will have good luck in the second, fourth, 11th, and 12th months of the Goat year. And they should make full use of their good luck in these four months. Monkey people will face many changed in their love affairs, and they should handle such situation cautiously in case of unnecessary disputes. Their spouses might become capricious, making Monkey people unhappy. The Monkey people born in summer will have bad luck. However, if these Monkey people could listen to others' opinions more often, their luck would turn better. In the Goat year, Monkey people are eager to do everything well, which might bring them troubles on the contrary. And they had better cultivate their moral characters.

属猴人遇猴年的流年运程
Fate of Monkey People in the Monkey Year

In the Monkey year, Monkey people will have up-and-down luck, but they will still feel happy. If they had few requirements, Monkey people could live through the year with ease. It is critical for Monkey people to remain open-minded in the Monkey year.

Monkey people are always not satisfied with their small success. They are often eager to defend what they have already achieved, and too aggressive to stay quietly. In fact, their most competent opponents are themselves. In the Monkey year, Monkey people should enrich their lives, not only clinging to their careers or make money, but also enjoying more family lives. More

Feng-Shui mascot monkey for happiness.

exercises and traveling will benefit their overall personal development. In the Monkey year, they should remain their head clear to distinguish who are their faithful friends.

The female Monkey people born in 1968 will have good luck in love affairs. They should step into new live phase with their dream lovers, avoiding missing good luck. The male Monkey people born in 1956 will also have good luck in love affairs. Among these Monkey people, married ones should keep away from paramours. Married Monkey people should travel with their spouses and enjoy their honeymoon again, play basketball, or go

swimming, learning calligraphy or cooking together. The Monkey year is a good year for Monkey people to receive further education.

In Jan. 1998, Central Africa Republic released a stamp of the Animal Signs in the first time.

属猴人遇鸡年的流年运程
Fate of Monkey People in the Rooster Year

Monkey people's luck in the Rooster year depends on their luck in the Monkey year. If they had bad luck in the Monkey year, everything would go well as they wish in the Rooster year, and they could get twice the result with half the effort. If they had good luck in the Monkey year, their luck in the Rooster year would become even better. If they had ordinary luck in the Monkey year, they would have better than average luck in the Rooster year.

In the Rooster year, Monkey people's career will be influenced by their affectional affairs. They should carefully balance their work and lives when working together with their spouses. The Monkey people who are employees will get promoted or get salary raises with the support of their supervisors. The Monkey people who are bosses will find everything goes well except for some arguments. In the Rooster year, Monkey people should make full use of their good luck to establish good relationships with others, and make friends with their opponents. In the Rooster year, Monkey people will make money from many resources. It is good time for Monkey people to try their best to earn and spend money. But they will only get little unexpected wealth, and have ordinary luck in gambling. The Rooster year is a year for Monkey people to face many challenges in affectional affairs. They should become more tolerant to their spouses in order to have harmonious lives. Unmarried Monkey people should be less subjective and more considerate for the other sides.

Feng-Shui mascot rooster for good luck.

73

属猴人遇狗年的流年运程
Fate of Monkey People in the Dog Year

In the Dog year, Monkey people will have ordinary luck with few auspicious stars but lots of ominous stars. Such situation indicates Monkey people will inevitably face many changes in the year. Thus, Monkey people should get prepared in advance for good opportunities in future. In short-term, the chaos is not auspicious. But in the lifetime of Monkey people, the Dog year is a year for Monkey people to experience difficulties and improve their capabilities. In the Dog year, with resolution and skills, Monkey people could go through difficulties without hurry-scurries.

The Dog year is a year to challenge Monkey people's personalities. Monkey people are born to be arrogant, aggressive, and energetic. Therefore, Monkey people will get ahead in adversities. In the Dog year, with great patience and endurance, Monkey people could no doubt turn corruption into magic.

In the aspects of career and wealth, the Monkey people born in 1956 will have good wealth luck in the Dog year. With the help of notable persons, the Monkey people born in 1944 will find good businesses opportunities. The Monkey people born in 1932 or 1968 will have bad luck. And the Monkey people born in 1980 will be involved into many troubles

and in bad relationships with others. In the Dog year, Monkey people should remain conservative rather than aggressive. The Dog year is a year for Monkey people to make lots of donations. In the Dog year, Monkey people should make friends extensively and do more charitable deeds with extended mercy. In the Dog year, Monkey people should practise more with few words. They are narrow-minded and eager to do well in everything. Monkey people would have a happy and peaceful year if they could act more while speaking less.

Feng-Shui mascot dog for wisdom.

属猴人遇猪年的流年运程
Fate of Monkey People in the Pig Year

Feng-Shui mascot pig for wealth.

Monkey people are born to be arrogant, aggressive, and energetic. Additionally, they always try to get ahead in every aspect. Thus, they could bring their potentials into full play in adversities. Monkey people are straightforward and indecisive to cut the knot. In the Pig year, it is more critical for Monkey people to control the overall situation and give good account of themselves without hesitation. It is the most important apocalypse for Monkey people in the Pig year.

In the aspecte of career and wealth, Monkey people will encounter bad luck and feel depressed in the Pig year. Therefore, it is important for Monkey people not to get into a dead end in the year. If they could remain positive and confident, and keep away from bad habits, Monkey people would make achievements in the Pig year.

In the Pig year, Monkey people will have good luck to get along well with others and perform excellently in challenging jobs. Specifically, female Monkey people will have even better luck than male ones. The Monkey people born in 1968 or 1980 will have good luck in examinations and writing. And their wealth luck will reach its summit in the third, 11th, and 12th months of the year. The Monkey people born in 1944 will have the best wealth luck in the Pig year among all Monkey people.

In the Pig year, Monkey people will have good luck to travel or migrate. Blesses by the auspicious stars "*yima*", they might stay in distant places for a long time. They will face many changes, including moving houses, changing jobs, or getting promoted, especially in the end of the Pig year.

12 属猴人守护神和本命年
Monkey People's Tutelary God and Animal Year

猴年出生者一生的守护神——大日如来佛
The Lifetime Tutelary God of Monkey People, Vairocana Buddha

Monkey people are gifted in make money. But they are imprudent and impaticent. Their tutelary god is Vairocana buddha, who is the supreme god in the esoteric branch of Buddhism. According to the Buddhist scripts, Vairocana bodhisattva has the power to enlighten all living things in the world. Therefore, by reverently enshrining Vairocana buddha, Mokey people could be enlightened, make great achievements with the help of notable persons.

本命年
Monkey People's Animal Year

Born in the Monkey year, these people have the Animal Sign of Monkey. And the Monkey year is their animal year, which comes in every 12 years.

Chinese think that one will be influenced by the year-god in one's animal year. The year-god indicates metabolism and dominates the change of one's luck. During the year, one would be in ups and downs ceaselessly. Since people always like stable and happy lives, they would worry about changes, whether good changes or bad, in their animal years.

According to Chinese *Feng-Shui* theory, in general, changes in one's animal year symbolize vitality, which might evolve into two different kinds of luck, good luck or bad. When in bad luck, one should learn how to give up and make use of those changes in one's animal years to adapt oneself to good opportunities in the next year. Additionally, one must keep away from dangers and stay safely in one's animal year.

At present, in China, people take account of their animal years that come in every 12 years. In the year, they will have something red on them. For example, both males and females will wear red underclothes, or take red lines on their wrists or waists. In China, people think red color could protect them from evils and bring them good luck. Moreover, some people who have more knowledge about *Feng-Shui* theory could take advantage of the changes in their animal years to enhance their luck, through praying to their tutelary gods in religion sites and adorning appropriate *Feng-Shui* mascots in their houses.

13 属猴人的五行助运物
Monkey People's *Feng-Shui* Mascots Related with the Five Elements

Many people are interested in how to dissolve their bad luck and enhance their good luck. In general, anything with pictures of rats, or dragons is good *Feng-Shui* mascots for Monkey people, and of great help to enhance their luck.

In the theory of the Five Elements, Monkey people have close relations with Rat people, or Dragon people. Their match will overwhelm other complementary and counteracting *Feng-Shui* factors. Therefore, it is appropriate for Monkey people to marry Rat people, Dragon people, or Pig people, who have good luck in the years when Monkey people have bad. By adorning a *Feng-Shui* mascots with pictures of rats, or dragons, or putting these mascots in auspicious places of their houses, Monkey people could take advantage of these mascots to go through difficulties. It is the simplest way of enhancing their luck. And Monkey people should always bear it in their minds.

Invested with marquis on horse.

属猴人的五行助运物

Monkey People's *Feng-Shui* Mascots Related with the Five Elements

风水助运鼠　　*Feng-Shui* Mascot Rat

In remote antiquity, since the beginning of history, a rat bit and separated the heaven and the earth. Consequently, *Zi*-Rat was endowed with vital forces between the heaven and the earth. Rat people would become notable persons and make great achievements. In Tibet Buddhism, rat symbolizes the Yellow God of Wealth, who holds a rat in the arm with a treasure bowl in front of him. He's the god dominating one's wealth luck. Additionally, with strong fecundity, rat is also regarded as a god who could bless people to have lots of offspring. By adorning a *Feng-Shui* mascots rat, one could make money and keep away from evils. By putting the mascots in his houses, one could get help of notable person and have good luck as well as lots of wealth and offspring.

Made of copper, jade, wood, or porcelain, *Feng-Shui* mascots are available in shops selling arts and crafts related with *Feng-Shui*. It is better if you pray in religion sites with your *Feng-Shui* mascots. In such way, your *Feng-Shui* mascots would be more powerful and bless you as you wish.

Feng-Shui mascot rat for good luck.

风水助运龙 *Feng-Shui* Mascot Dragon

Dragon is the culture totem of Chinese people, holding a supreme position in Chinese culture. It concentrates the quintessence of Chinese culture with the history of thousands of years, and is the symbol of sovereign power. Dragon people are born to be leaders, with subtle perception, unparallel courage, great foresight, distinguished wisdom, and uncommon manners. When adorned on one's body or in one's house, *Feng-Shui* mascots dragon should be oriented to face seas or rivers. The mascots could dissolve bad luck and bring good luck to people.

A coiling dragon bringing in treasures.

On Jan. 1, 1992, North Korea released stamps of the Monkey year. The design adopted a literary quotation about a monkey in Chinese history. It is said that when Heng Wen, great general of Eastern Jin Dynasty, led his troops go through Changjiang river by water, one of his soldiers caught a little monkey in the bank of the river and brought it to the boat. However, the mother monkey followed the boat for hundreds of miles, wailing for its child. And finally, the mother monkey jumped into the boat from a cliff and died. Someone in the troop anatomized the dead monkey and found its intestines had been broken up into pieces. Hengwen was very angry about his soldiers' behavior and dismissed the soldier.

14

本命卦和八种宅卦
Divinatory Symbols of One's Animal Year and Eight Kinds of Divinatory Symbols of Buildings

In China, there is a fantastic book called *Yijing* that has 3000 years of history. With this book, one could predict his or her fate according to one's birthday. The graph below is ranked according to *Yijing*. One can find the divinatory symbols of one's animal year, and understand one's auspicious or ominous *Feng-Shui* orientations in the eight divinatory symbols. The graph is very critical for people to change one's fate.

本命卦一览表
The List of Divinatory Symbols of One's Animal Year

Men	Dui	Qian	Kun	Xun	Zhen	Kun	Kan	Li	Gen
Women	Gen	Li	Kan	Kun	Zhen	Xun	Kun	Qian	Dui
Birth Year	1921	1922	1923	1924	1925	1926	1927	1928	1929
Birth Year	1930	1931	1932	1933	1934	1935	1936	1937	1938
Birth Year	1939	1940	1941	1942	1943	1944	1945	1946	1947
Birth Year	1948	1949	1950	1951	1952	1953	1954	1955	1956
Birth Year	1957	1958	1959	1960	1961	1962	1963	1964	1965
Birth Year	1966	1967	1968	1969	1970	1971	1972	1973	1974
Birth Year	1975	1976	1977	1978	1979	1980	1981	1982	1983
Birth Year	1984	1985	1986	1987	1988	1989	1990	1991	1992
Birth Year	1993	1994	1995	1996	1997	1998	1999	2000	2001
Birth Year	2002	2003	2004	2005	2006	2007	2008	2009	2010
Birth Year	2011	2012	2013	2014	2015	2016	2017	2018	2019
Birth Year	2020	2021	2022	2023	2024	2025	2026	2027	2028
Birth Year	2029	2030	2031	2032	2033	2034	2035	2036	2037
Birth Year	2038	2039	2040	2041	2042	2043	2044	2045	2046
Birth Year	2047	2048	2049	2050	2051	2052	2053	2054	2055

Everyone has the divinatory symbols of one's animal year once he or she is born.

(The year in the list refers to a year in the lunar calendar. For the detailed lunar calendar, please see "Specification of the Five Elements for the twelve Animal Signs". Pay attention that males and females born in the same lunar year have different divinatory symbols!)

本命卦吉凶方位盘
Orientation Panels of Good or Bad Luck in Divinatory
Symbols for One's Birth Year

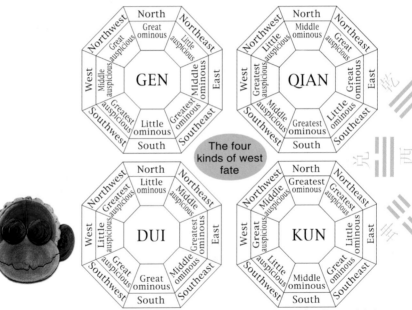

If the divinatory symbol of one's animal year appears as *Qian, Kun, Dui,* or *Gen* diagram, it belongs to the four kinds of west fate. And one's auspicious stars would appear in the west, southwest, northwest, or northeast, while one's ominous stars would appear in the east, south, north, or southeast.

The four kinds of east fate

Qian, Kun, Dui, Zhen, Kan, Xun, Gen: the eight words represent eight fixed divinatory directions to predict one's fate.

If the divinatory symbol of one's animal year appears as *Zhen, Xun, Kan,* or *Li* diagram, it belongs to the four kinds of east fate. And one's auspicious stars would appear in the east, southeast, south, or north, while one's ominous stars would appear in the southwest, west, northwest, or northeast.

八种宅卦（家宅和办公室）
Eight Kinds of Divinatory Symbols of Buildings (Including Houses or Working Places)

In Chinese *Feng-Shui* theory, there are eight kinds of divinatory symbols of any building based on the orientations of the building's gate. The eight kinds include *Zhen* building, *Xun* building, *Kan* building, *Li* building, *Qian* building, *Kun* building, *Gen* building, and *Dui* building.

Zhen building has its gate opened to the west.

Dui building has its gate opened to the east.

Li building has its gate opened to the north.

Kan building has its gate opened to the south.

Xun building has its gate opened to the northwest.

Qian building has its gate opened to the southeast.

Kun building has its gate opened to the northeast.

Gen building has its gate opened to the southwest.

Zhen building, *Xun* building, *Kan* building, and *Li* building are called the four kinds of east buildings, whose auspicious stars would appear in the east, southeast, south, or north, and whose ominous stars would appear in the west, southwest, northwest, or northeast.

Qian building, *Kun* building, *Dui* building, and *Gen* building are called the four kinds of west buildings, whose auspicious stars would appear in the west, southwest, northwest, or northeast, and whose ominous stars would appear in the east, south, north, or southeast.

In Chinese *Feng-Shui* theory, it is auspicious if the divinatory symbols of one's animal year and of one's houses have similar auspicious or ominous omens. Therefore, it is obvious that people with the four kinds of east fate should live in the four kinds of east buildings, while people with the four kinds of west fate should live in the four kinds of west buildings. It is the divinatory symbols of the housemaster's animal year that decides whether the divinatory symbols of one's animal year and of one's houses will enhance or counteract with each other.

If people with the four kinds of east fate live in the four kinds of west buildings, or people with the four kinds of west fate live in the four kinds of east buildings, it indicates that these people's Five Elements would counteract with each other. However, their bad luck could be weakened by rearrange the Five Elements in their houses. For example, by putting a piece of calligraphy and painting, or a *Feng-Shui* mascot such as *Kylin, Longgui, Pixiu* in the ominous orientations of the houses, these people could exorcise evil spirits with evil forces, therfore balancing the Five Elements.

In order to hold one's fate, it is necessary and important to understand the eight *Feng-Shui* orientations in the divinatory symbols of one's animal year and of one's houses. The knowledge is also the focus of this book.

On Jan. 22, 1992, China released a stamp of the Monkey year. In Chinese folk customs, Peach is the symbol of longevity. In Chinese myth, there is a peach garden in the Heaven. And peach is an important food in the birthday party of Wangmu, the queen of the Heaven. Additionally, people always connect monkey with peach.

15 风水旺位的确定和风水吉祥物的运用
Auspicious *Feng-Shui* Orientations and Typical *Feng-Shui* Mascots

Door-god.

In summary, Chinese *Feng-Shui* theory emphasizes the investigation of local climates and geographical environments including geology, hydrology, ecology, and landscapes. Furthermore, the theory tries to find ways to adapt these factors to human beings' requirements of living, creating a perfect, auspicious, and harmonious circumstance between the universe and human beings. The theory is also a practical technique for Chinese people to refine their environments and improve their life qualities.

The foundation of Chinese *Feng-Shui* theory includes *Bagua*, *Yin-Yang*, and the Five Elements. Chinese ancestors invent *Bagua* through looking up to the heaven and looking down to the earth, studying everything on earth, and digging into innermost beings of themselves. Although *Bagua* only has eight Triagrams, in fact it includes everything and has close relations with *Yin-Yang* and the Five Elements. If the Five Elements complemented with each other, the world would be happy and peaceful. On the other hand, if the Five Elements counteracted with each other, there would appear many misfortunes and disasters in the world. Ominous divinatory symbols of one's house represent the coming of troubles in one's marriage, and perhaps ill wealth luck and bad health. Practices of *Feng-Shui* try to discover defects of the Five Elements related with one's house or working place, and rearrange the divinatory symbols in order to turn ill luck into good. By such way, one could not only have comfortable residence or working environments, but also enjoy a happy life and a successful career.

All layouts of a room can be explained by *Feng-Shui* theory. Augurs who are good at *Feng-Shui* theory could turn corruption into magic and ill luck into good by putting *Feng-Shui* mascots in appropriate places. On the other hand, if one ignored invisible evil omens from outside world, one would run into troubles.

Feng-Shui is a theory to change one's fate in pursuit of happiness. It is a kind of wisdom on how to make use of various *Feng-Shui* mascots, locations, or colors to improve environments, dispel bad luck, and enhance happiness.

Door-god.

风水吉祥物的运用
Typical *Feng-Shui* Mascots

If living in one's own house, one could select appropriate *Feng-Shui* mascots according to the auspicious or ominous omens in the divinatory symbols of the house. If living in a rent apartment, one could select appropriate *Feng-Shui* mascots according to the auspicious or ominous omens in the divinatory symbols of one's animal year. *Feng-Shui* mascots are very important to change one's fate.

① 武财神——关公
The military god of wealth - Guangong

Guangong was originally called Guan Yunchang in Chinese, who was a sworn brother of Liu Bei and Zhang Fei, and a famous general in the era of the Three kingdoms (220-265 AD) in China. With great loyalty and dignity, he would rather die than betray his sworn brothers. Admiring his loyalty and credit, business persons regard Guangong as the military god of wealth. By putting his statue in houses or stores, they were announcing that they would be as faithful and honest as Guangong. With mutual trust, they will have successful businesses and make lots of money. As the military god of wealth, Guangong can bring people peace and good luck to make money, and exorcise evil spirits from houses. It is appropriate to put his statues in houses, working places, or stores. The statues should face outside to the gate of the buildings in order to bring in wealth and riches, and to protect from evils.

② 貔貅——最好风水物
Pixiu - one of the best *Feng-Shui* mascots

Pixiu are so fierce as to deter enemies, but loyal to its masters. With string force, it can dispel various kinds of evils including *Fanguang, Liandao, Qiang, Chuanxin, Tianqiao, Chong, Sheng, Cimian, Wei,* and *Liunian. Pixiu* has 26 kinds of shapes. The twenty-six evil spirits of *Pixiu* are twenty-six phenomena of architectural environment, which form a kind of harmful trends. Chinese people think that these evil spirits are bad murderous looks. *Pixiu* has long nose, wings, and hair all over its body. Without an asshole, it has foods but never evacuate, which indicates that wealth will come but never go. With kind nature, *Pixiu* loves children very much, thus bringing peace to families. So *Pixiu* is a very good *Feng-Shui* mascot suitable for businesspersons, managers trying to get along well with others, salespeople, or people interested in horse racing or *Liuhe* lottery. Generally, it will especially benefit those people without stable income. But one should prevent others from touching his or her *Feng-Shui* mascot *Pixiu* in case of losing good wealth luck.

It is suitable to put the mascot in the lobby of one's house or bedroom with its mouth toward the door or window. Moreover, it is even better to put mother and child *Pixius* together. Many people who have *Feng-Shui* mascot *Pixiu* said that it could deter evils far and near.

3 文财神——福、禄、寿三星

The civil gods of wealth - the three gods of *Fu*, *Lu*, and *Shou*.

With a baby on arms, the god of *Fu* will bring good luck to every one so that he or she would have lots offspring and everything would go well as he or she wishes. Dressing fineries and with a jade scepter on hand, the god of *Lu* will bless people to get promoted and make money. With a peach on hand and smile on face, the god of *Shou* symbolizes longevity. In the very beginning, among the three gods, only the god of *Lu* was regarded as the god of wealth. However, the three gods always appear as a trinity, which represents good health, longevity, and great power. Thus, the gods of *Fu* and *Shou* are also regarded as the gods of wealth.

The statues of the civil gods of wealth should be oriented to different directions from that of the military god of wealth. The three gods of *Fu*, *Lu*, and *Shou* should be oriented toward inside houses, otherwise the good luck of wealth and power would be given outside. It is good to put the civil gods of wealth in offices or houses.

4 风水字画——最佳风水物

Feng-Shui calligraphies and paintings - one of the best *Feng-Shui* mascots

One could make an auspicious and magnificent atmosphere in offices, hotels, or houses by decorating *Feng-Shui* calligraphies and paintings in these buildings. The paintings could not only demonstrate the cultural tastes of the householders, but also impress and enrich the audience with beautiful images of

seas, mountains, rivers, pines, or willows. Additionally, the paintings are helpful to the health of the audiences' bodies and minds. It could make perfection still more perfect if one put calligraphies with best wishes in room. Good *Feng-Shui* paintings often have auspicious figures on paper, such as Buddha, goats, mandarin ducks, horses, carps, cranes, and clouds.

Feng-Shui paintings could be put in the eight orientations in offices or houses to change one's fates. For example, the paintings of carps hung in the auspicious orientations of the divinatory symbols of one's animal year would bring good luck, while those of Zhongkui hung in the ominous orientations would deter evils. At present, calligraphies and paintings are in great demand in Chinese cultural market, and their values have been increased a lot. Moreover, it is expected that their prices will increase more in near future.

⑤ 麒麟——万能的灵兽
Kylin - omnipotent divine animal

Kylin, as well as dragon, phoenix, and tortoise are regarded as the Four Divine animals in ancient times. *Feng-Shui* mascot *Kylin* could bring people good wealth luck and dissolve evils. Put in one's house with its face toward outside, it could bring the householder good luck to get promoted, make money, or have lots of offspring.

It is good to put *Feng-Shui* mascot *Kylin* in both auspicious and ominous orientations of the divinatory symbols of one's house, with its face toward outside of the room. Additionally, it is suitable to choose small-sized or middle-sized, metal statues of *Kylin*.

6 狮子——强势瑞兽

Lion - the powerful auspicious animal

Lion is the most powerful auspicious animal who can drive out various evils and strengthen the power of companies, banks, office buildings, and shopping malls. In the past, many rich families often put a pair of stone lions in the front of gates in order to enhance their good luck and have everything going well as they wish. If an office building were in bad environments, such as the window of one's room faced toward something with pointed shape, it would be better to put a pair of little porcelain lions facing outside of the window. In Chinese tradition, it is said that for those people whose professional depend primarily on eloquence, such as lawyers, play-actors, or attendants, it is better to put a pair of stone or porcelain lions in the front of the gates of their offices or houses. In such way, these people would have good luck to get promoted, make money, or gain reputations.

With great masculinities, middle-sized or big-sized bronze or stone lions could be used to protect one's house from evils. The statues should be put in both sides outside of gate with the lions' mouths toward outside.

It would bring good wealth luck for Water people to choose bronze lions since according to the Five Elements theory, the Metal could enhance the Water.

93

7 龙龟——制煞利兽

Dragon tortoise - the divine animal detering evils

Dragon tortoise is a kind of auspicious divine animals that brings good wealth luck and guard against villains. Moreover, it can bring people good luck to get along with others and protect people from unexpected hurts or troubles.

By putting a *Feng-Shui* mascot dragon tortoise in one's house or working place, one could make money and have a successful career. Additionally, it should be put in the most ominous orientations of the divinatory symbols of a building.

8 三脚蟾蜍——大众发财兽
The toad with three legs-
the wealth animal for common people

It is said that the toad has three legs, seven stars on back, two bunches of coins in mouth, *Taiji* diagrams on head, and odd-shaped gold under feet. The Animal is the best *Feng-Shui* mascot for enhancing wealth luck. Different from normal kind of toads with four legs, it was a spirit that later had surrendered to the supernatural being Liuhai, thereafter giving up evil and returning to good, and helping the poor all over the world. Gradually, it has become a wealth animal for common people.

By adorning a *Feng-Shui* mascot toad, poor people would have better income. Specifically, it should be put in the two most auspicious orientations of one's house, with its mouth toward inside of the house. Otherwise, the good wealth luck would flow out of the house.

9 水晶物——宇宙的神秘力量

Crystal - mysterious power of the universe

Crystal has a kind of mysterious power since it could aggregate energy from spaces nearby. Put in the most auspicious orientation of the divinatory symbols of buildings, crystal could bring people good luck to get promoted and make much money. By putting it in study rooms, one could get excellent grades in study. By putting it in the corners of offices, one could have a clearer mind in business. Or by it putting it in kids' rooms, one could improve one's children's interest in reading and studying.

10 屏风影壁——实用的风水吉物
Screen wall - useful *Feng-Shui* mascot

According to Chinese *Feng-Shui* theory, without a screen wall, Qi (flow of energy) would come and go straightforwardly. On the other hand, with a screen wall, Qi would go around the screen in a S-shape route. In every yard of the Forbidden City, Beijing, there are screens made of bricks, woods, or jade.

Screen walls could slow down Qi and make people feel comfortable, which is helpful to both health and careers of any people.

Moreover, folding screen walls are flexible and easy to place, and could ward off evils from various directions. Besides these functions, calligraphies and paintings on folding screen walls could please people. With their functional and sensual features, folding screen walls are auspicious mascots helpful to rearrange indoor *Feng-Shui* omens.

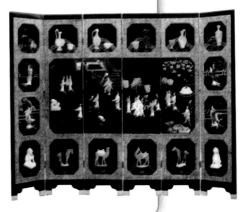

11 古钱——增财引子
Acient coins - introduction of wealth

Tian Xi Tong Bao copper coin.

Jing You Yuan Bao copper coin.

Jia Qing Tong Bao copper coin.

Tian Sheng Yuan Bao copper coin.

Huang Song Tong Bao copper coin.

Qian Long Tong Bao copper coin.

Tian Sheng Yuan Bao copper coin.

Huang Song Tong Bao copper coin.

Qian Long Bei Qian copper coin.

As the introduction of wealth, acient coins could bring people good luck to make expected or unexpected wealth. One general principle is that things of the same kind will come together. Besides the value as cultural relic, acient coins could bring people more wealth with very good luck accumulated by generations of acients people.

It is good to put acient coins in the three most aupicious orientations of the divinatory symbols of buildings.

Kang Xi Tong Bao copper coin.

12 文昌塔——功名神物
Wenchang tower - mascot for career successes

Wenchang tower is a common mascot that could bring people good luck in study and career development. In the area of Yuan Lang Ping Mountain, there have appeared many famous scholars and goverment officials because there are some *Wenchang* towers built in the area. By putting *Wenchang* towers at the end of beds, on desks, or in bookshelves, people could become more creative and intelligent, therefore making great achievements.

13 葫芦——健康宝物
Calabash - mascot for health

It is said that calabash is effective to help people get rid of diseases and recover quickly. *Feng-Shui* mascot calabash could be made of natural calabash, bronze, wood, or porcelain. Put in the three most auspicious orientations in one's house, it could bless one's family with good health.

14 观世音菩萨——万灵的菩萨
Guanyin - efficacious Bodhisattva

Guanyin Bodhisattva is efficacious to relieve others' hardships and sufferings. Therefore, in China, almost all families have statues of Guanyin in their houses.

According to Buddhist scripts, long before Sakyamuni was enlightened, Guanyin had been a Buddha, who transformed herself into a Bodhisattva in order to enlighten people all over the world.

It is said that Guanyin Bodhisattva can bless one's family with safety and health. With its statue in one's house, one can have a harmonious family and a successful life, and go through any difficulty.

With tolerant character and merciful heart, Guanyin Bodhisattva devote herself into the task of relieving others' suffering and bringing happiness to every person.

One should burn a joss stick in every morning and evening when praying at Guanyin Bodhisattva, and replace offering fruits periodically. Moreover, one would have better luck and a happier life if he or she had the replaced offering fruits.

The Guanyin Bodhisattva with a thousand arms, Tangka, Qing Dynasty (1644-1911AD).

15 大肚弥勒佛——布袋和尚
Mitreya Buddha - the Monk with a bag

Mitreya Buddha's name is Qici and his alias is Changtingzi in Chinese. He was a monk in Later Liang of the Five Dynasties in China. With plump body and fat belly, he could forecast cloudy or sunny weathers as well as others fates. He was often found begging alms in downtowns with a big bag. And it is strange that his bag was never full. In 917 A.D., he passed away in *Yanlin* temple. Later, people knew the fat monk was Mitreya Buddha, also called the Monk with a bag. He is famous for his great tolerance by tolerating everything and smiling at everyone in the world. Now, his statues are often found in companies and stores.

By putting the statue of Mitreya Buddha in the center of lobbies of office buildings, one could have good luck of wealth and career, while everything will go well as one wishes.

16 怎样掌握调理自身运程
How to Hold and Rearrange One's Fate

Everything has its reason and there are gods above one's head. In all ages, there are many fantastic events that couldn't be explained by modern sciences. In the 15th century, Tycho, the great astrologist, said astrology had its solid foundation and is compatible with various kinds of religions. And there were many examples showing that one had predestinate fate upon his or her birth. However, one's fate could be changed by one's will power and hard working. Moreover, Tycho said the wisest ones could dominate their destinies though most people could not control their fates. In order to change their fates into better ones, people should not only depend on religions and gods, but also make efforts and work hard with a kind and tolerant heart.

Chinese *Feng-Shui* theory tries to rearrange people's fates in pursuit of the harmony between the nature and human beings. It advocates people should respect their inner motivations and feelings

Feng-Shui Mascots of Animal Signs.

in order to live happy lives. People could not enjoy their good luck without healthy bodies and minds. Now, there are some astrologists emphasizing too much on minor details and rigid rules, which might confuse most people. Thus, it is a good suggestion that one should care about primary *Feng-Shui* factors, such as the divinatory symbols of one's animal year and houses, as well as the relationships between one's fate and the divinatory symbols. Specifically, one should arrange one's home or office according to one's own interesting. The good designs are those in which one feels comfortable and happy. If one felt uncomfortable about a house, one could put some *Feng-Shui* mascots in the house, or consult *Feng-Shui* experts for help.

In near future, the author will release the book "*Inside Chinese Feng-Shui Theory and Auspicious Omens*" for readers who have further interests in Chinese *Feng-Shui* theory.

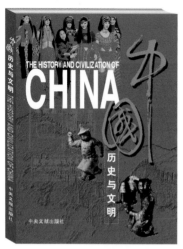

英文版《中国历史与文明》全新大制作

全书涵盖自原始社会到 2002 年的中华文明史——

纵览古今政治风云 领略华夏社会风情

探寻华夏历史遗址 鉴赏华夏文物瑰宝

一册在手

走遍中国

洞晓古今

2003 年优秀外文图书